2018
TAX REFORMS

And What It Really Means For You

A Complete Guide to How the New
Law can Affect an Average American
Like us !

C D LEONARD

The Tax Cut and Jobs Act
What Middle America Needs to Know

The Tax Cut and Jobs Act is the most drastic change to Tax law in decades

What does it all mean?

Table of Contents

What is the law? A brief
What was the problem
What does the new law do / require?
What does this mean for Jack and Jill?
…and Andreas
Misconceptions/ Criticisms/ Clarification
Expert tips

Chapter 7 : Increase in Estate and Gift Tax Exemption

What is the law? A brief
What was the problem
What does the new law do / require?
What does this mean for Jack and Jill?
Misconceptions/ Criticisms/ Clarification
Expert tips

Chapter 8 : Extension of Time Limit for contesting IRS Levy

What is the law? A brief
What was the problem
What does the new law do / require?
What does this mean for Jack and Jill Enterprises? (and Andreas Coffee Shop as well)
Misconceptions/ Criticisms/ Clarification
Expert tips

Chapter 9 : Deduction for Qualified Business Income of Pass-Through Entities

What is the law? A brief
What was the problem
What does the new law do / require?
What does this mean for Jack and Jill Enterprises? (and Andreas Coffee Shop as well)
Misconceptions/ Criticisms/ Clarification
Expert tips

Chapter 10 : Business Losses and Net Operating Losses (NOLS) for Corporate and Non-Corparate Taxpayers.

What is the law? A brief
What was the problem
What does the new law do / require?
What does this mean for Jack and Jill Enterprises? (and Andreas Coffee Shop as well)
Misconceptions/ Criticisms/ Clarification
Expert tips

Chapter 11 : Elimination of the Secion 199 Deduction

What is the law? A brief
What was the problem?
What does the new law do / require?
What does this mean for Jack and Jill Enterprises? (and Andreas Coffee Shop as well)
Misconceptions/ Criticisms/ Clarification
Expert tips

Chapter 12 : Changes to Executive Compensation for Publicly Held Entities/ Companies/ Organisations – Section 162(M)

What is the law? A brief
What was the problem
What does the new law do / require?
What does this mean for Jack and Jill Enterprises? (and Andreas Coffee Shop as well)
Misconceptions/ Criticisms/ Clarification
Expert tips

Chapter 13 : New Measures of Inflation

What is the law? A brief
What was the problem
What does the new law do / require?
What does this mean for Jack and Jill Enterprises? (and Andreas Coffee Shop as well)
Misconceptions/ Criticisms/ Clarification
Expert tips

Chapter 14 : Doubling of The Expensing Limit Under Section 179

What is the law? A brief
What was the problem
What does the new law do / require?
What does this mean for Jack and Jill Enterprises? (and Andreas Coffee Shop as well)
Misconceptions/ Criticisms/ Clarification
Expert tips

Chapter 15 : Other Provisions

What is the law? A brief
What was the problem
What does the new law do / require?
What does this mean for Jack and Jill Enterprises? (and Andreas Coffee Shop as well)
Misconceptions/ Criticisms/ Clarification
Expert tips

Bibliography

<u>Copyright</u>

Preface

The recent tax changes were rushed through Congress and the Senate, there was a minimum of debate and public oversight, so it's very hard to know the implications of these changes.

The last thing you need is to spend your time reading dense legislation, so that's been done for you and condensed and simplified into this eBook.

This eBook debunks the myths surrounding the changes, laying out where the advantages and disadvantages are of the legislation are, and what to do about it to get the best for you and your family. Income tax, corporate tax, benefits and every other area of the new laws are all covered in clear, easy to understand language.

<u>Disclaimer</u>

PART I

Chapter 1 : Book Introduction

The Tax Cut and Jobs Act is the most drastic change to Tax Law in decades

What does it all mean?

The current Tax Cut and Jobs Act ('the TCJA') that was recently passed into law has been hotly debated, with various political and popular opinions dominating the media in 2016 and 2017. Senator Mitch McConnell, the majority leader, heralded that the tax bill was a sign that government had 'heard' middle class Americans. However, despite the TCJA cutting tax rates for the majority of payers, the passing of the law has been a journey fraught with opposition.

For some, there is a belief that the reform only benefits big corporations and the wealthy. For the majority, it is most likely the so-called complexity of the new regulations, that is challenging. Nonetheless, supporters believe the bill will give the economy stimulus.

The purpose of this book is to provide a "how to" of the TCJA for people earning between $35,000 and $100,000 per year. The massive reform has been lauded as a response to the needs of middle America, but does it deliver.

The book is divided into nine substantive sections.

- PART I – Tax rate reform

- PART II – Tax Benefits for Families and Individuals

- PART III – Education

- PART IV – Deductions and Exclusions

- PART V – Increase in Estate and Gift Tax Exemptions

- PART VI – Extension of time limit for contesting IRS levy

- PART VII – Deduction for qualified business income of pass-thru entities

- PART VIII – Business Losses and Net Operating Losses (NOLS) for Corporate and Non – Corporate Taxpayers.

- PART IX – Other provisions (this part will be more detailed as the book goes on)

A brief historical introduction

President Donald Trump got his first significant win as the President of the United States and leader of the Republican party by signing a new tax bill into law. Trump coined it the "Tax Cuts and Jobs Act", a euphemism for the good things he promises the bill will bring for America (Floyd, 2018).

In summary, the bill has sweeping reforms to the current tax systems, reducing the income rate tax, corporate rate taxes, as well as other significant reforms causing divides amongst many leaders in public and private sectors. The primary point of contention splitting the two parties revolves around whether the law cuts taxes for those that are already wealthy, even though all parties agree in public that they do not want to pass a bill that does exactly that.

Critics argue that cuts to corporate taxes, and reducing the top personal income tax rate from 39.6% to 33% (Burman et al., 2017, pp. 262) will only favor persons already in the highest tax band ranges. The fairly strong rebuttal has been to deny such a view, and argue that reductions would be felt at every tax band. The question appears to be how much will the cuts actually trickle down[1] to benefit wider America. Vice President Mike Pence believes that the effect will be strong and apparent. The politician seemed to affirm that the law was a Christmas gift to all Americans, choosing to comment by quipping, "Merry Christmas, America". The tax deductions promoted here are technically true, but these assertions do not address the differences in reductions to people across bands, meaning that some people have bigger tax cuts than others.

Let's us evaluate some of the most drastic changes to the law that has just been repealed.

---

[1]   See Tickle-Down Theory

PART I

Chapter 2 : Tax Rate Reform - Corporate Tax

Introduction to Tax Rate Reforms in terms of Corporate Tax

What is the law? A brief

Corporate taxes are taxes levied at corporations, as you might have guessed. Such tax can be payable to at the local, state and federal levels in the United States. It is a fairly complicated system as each state can have a different tax rate, Iowa, Minnesota, and Alaska have tax on gross receipts over 9% whereas in Texas and Nevada such tax is absent.

Nonetheless, it is the federal level that poses the most significant taxes on corporations.

Corporate Tax – Flat Rate

The corporate tax rate has been changed to a flat 21% starting 1 January 2018 after the passage of the TCJA

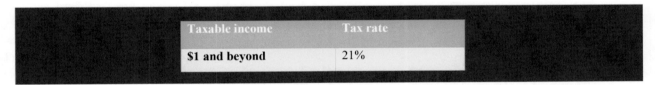

Taxable income	Tax rate
$1 and beyond	21%

The old law

The repealed law works by specifying a specific payable amount for a corporation to pay within specific earning bands, with excess payments paid on the excess of the lower limit of that band (PWC, 2017). Essentially, tax bands work within your earnings category. Below is a table of a typical portion of the outgoing law, but is still a good example.

Outgoing tax brackets table

Over (USD*)	But not over (USD*)	Pay (USD)+	% on excess	of the amount over (USD*)
-	50,000	-	15	
50,000	75,000	7,500	25	50,000
75,000	100,000	13,750	34	75,000
100,000	335,000	22,250	39	100,000
335,000	10,000,000	113,900	34	335,000
10,000,000	15,000,000	3,400,000	35	10,000,000
15,000,000	18,333,333	5,150,000	38	15,000,000
18,333,333		-	35	-

Source: pwc (2017)

Using this table, one could calculate the standard corporate tax by using the band that a business falls in on the left-hand side of the table (pWc, 2017). Therefore, for example, if your business falls under the $75,000 - $100,000, you would pay a rate of $ 13,750 as the standard tax, plus a 34% tax on any amount above the lower end of the tax band, which is anything above $75,000.

Back to our example. If you then had an income before tax of $ 90,000, you would first pay the $13,750, and then calculate the excess. Excess would be calculating by deducting the $ 90,000 you earned from the lower end of the band $ 75,000 ($90,000 - $75,000 = $15,000). We then take 34% of $15,000 (our excess), which is $5,100. Add the initial pay of $13,750 to the $5,100 of excess tax and we have our total tax amount of $18,850. This means that if your business earned $90,000 in income under the old tax law, then you would pay $18,850 in taxes. A summary of this is below.

Example of tax calculation

Net income	90,000	
Payable tax	13,750	
Excess	15,000	*$90,000 - $ 75,000
34% of excess	5,100	
Total tax	18,850	

Source: computation. *Note that this may not include some specific standard deductions

The US corporate income tax (CIT) is based on a progressive tax rates, meaning that they tax rates increase with higher income earned. However, there exists a parallel tax system called the Alternative Minimum Tax (AMT) that provides for stricter taxes on companies by reducing the number of deductions (think of these as items that can reduce tax). A reduction on the possible deductions means that companies could not use the system to reduce their tax bill.

What was the problem

From a tax perspective, the law that came before the TCJA meant that companies had to either pay the corporate tax rate, or the AMT rate, whichever was higher (Anderson Kill, 2018). The argument against these taxes is that because they were so high, they acted to dis-incentivise companies from setting up or staying in America, thus moving jobs away from the economy. President Trump had argued that under the tax bill, "our companies won't be leaving our country any longer."

> *"our companies won't be leaving our country any longer." - President Donald Trump*

Therefore, by lowering taxes, supporters[1], argue that companies will have more reasons to stay or set up in the country, meaning that they would create jobs. As an added bonus, they also argue that the extra cash generated by corporations through this tax cuts would potentially increase wages for workers, as well as potential work-related benefits.

What does the new law do/ require?

The new law, first and foremost, repealed the AMT system (Anderson Kill, 2018). This would mean that corporations cannot use specific tax credits/exemptions that they could use for the normal tax rates. By using the AMT system, some taxpayers could take advantage by using deductibles that would be allowable for the AMT system, but not for the normal tax system. Since the requirement for those that qualify for the AMT system is that they compute both their normal tax dues and their AMT tax dues, and then pay whichever of the two is higher, they would have no way to benefit from paying lower taxes in such a situation. The effect is that a repeal of these taxes means that only the standard corporate tax is used, and thus companies can adjust their income downwards by using these credits as deductions, thus reducing their taxable amount. The new taxable amount is a flat rate of 21% on net income. Therefore, a corporation that earned, like in the previous example, a net income of $ 90,000, would be subject to only a 21% tax. Effectively, this would mean that the company would pay 21% of $ 90,000, which is $ 18,900.

Alternative example of tax calculation	
Net income	$ 90,000
21% tax rate	$ 18,900
Total tax	$ 18,900

Source: computation

---

[1] The law had mostly Republican support in the House and the Senate.

You will notice, that under TCJA, tax would increase by around $ 50 for a company earning $ 90,000. However, for companies with higher net incomes, overall taxes paid by that company will fall. Take for example a company under the old law and TCJA below:

Comparison of higher income company			
Company earning $ 12,000,000 a year			
Old law		New law	
Net income	$12,000,000	Net income	$ 12,000,000
Payable tax	$ 3,400,000	21% tax rate	$ 2,520,000
Excess	$ 2,000,000		-
35% of excess	$ 700,000		-
Total tax	$ 4,100,000	Total tax	$ 2,520,000
Net savings	$ 1,580,000		

Source: computation

As per table 4, a company earning net income $ 12,000,000 would benefit by $1,580,000 in additional cash due to lower taxes paid when compared to the older law.

What does this mean for Jack and Jill?

Assume two companies here. Jack and Jill Enterprises (J&J) with a large net income (income less all business costs), and the second company is Andreas Coffee Shop that operates out of a small town.

Also, assume that, as per the example, Jack and Jill earn around $12 million per year. As calculated, the old system would tax require J&J to pay a tax amount of around $4.1 million for the year. With TCJA, the same company with would pay a significantly lower amount totaling $2.52 million, freeing up $1.58 million for the company. J&J can use this freed up capital for many uses, some of which include business expansion through increased investment, employee rewards schemes and wage increments, and increase shareholder wealth. Therefore, through increased savings, the federal government expects that such companies will then increase their capital expenditure, and also improve their employees' affairs by increasing their spending ability.

...and Andreas

For a company on the lower end of the net income for the year, for example, Andreas Coffee Shop (ACS), with a net income of $ 90,000, the TCJA will increase taxes by $50 as earlier alluded. However, this is marginal and can be considered insignificant in the grand scale of things.

J&J, as well as ACS, would also benefit from 'full expensing' for investments under TCJA (Bowman, 2017). This is just fancy talk for being able to deduct any investment costs made from your taxes. Spend $10,000 on a new machine to help make better coffee, and ACS can deduct this from their tax bill, making them $10,000. Therefore, this is an incentive for businesses to invest in expanding their business with capital intensive investments.

Overall, the tax regime offers tremendous advantages. However, there some misconceptions about changes. One key criticism of the TCJA is that it is likely to increase the federal deficit, especially since the corporations will likely pay lower taxes, thereby reducing collections of taxes by the US government. The country is already at a deficit as it is, paying 43% of its total spending by borrowing (Rugy, 2011). The government has run on a deficit from 1980-1997, continuing with the trend from 2001 onward. Current estimates are that the deficit is likely to expand by $1.5 trillion by the year 2028, a situation that could potentially mean that the total debt owed by the US would exceed the size of the economy (CRFB, 2017). Of this $1.5 trillion, around $1 trillion would come from business taxes, meaning that business tax cuts would account for 67% of the total deficit growth.

A fairly strong counter to the assertion is that the economy would grow faster than the deficit, especially due to expected increased investment and spending by companies benefiting from these tax cuts. The GOP believe that this would therefore lead to higher collections by the government, thus making up for the deficit that the cuts exposed the country to by increasing their collections as a result of the general populace accumulating more wealth, moving higher up in tax brackets, and thusly paying more taxes. Higher taxes would then narrow or negate the deficit caused by the tax cuts. The validity of these claims is unverifiable for the most part, especially since this is partisan issue, and it may be difficult to ascertain which estimates presented by either side. Below is an excerpt of a letter written by 137 economists that support the GOP tax plan:

> *Dear Senators and Representatives,*
>
> *"Ask five economists," as the Edgar Fiedler adage goes, "and you'll get five different answers."*
>
> *Yet, when it comes to the tax reform package aimed at fixing our broken system, the undersigned have but one shared perspective: Economic growth will accelerate if the Tax Cuts and Jobs Act passes, leading to more jobs, higher wages, and a better standard of living for the American people. If, however, the bill fails, the United States risks continued economic under-performance... We firmly believe that a competitive corporate rate is the key to an economic engine driven by greater investment, capital stock, business formation, and productivity - all of which will yield more jobs and higher wages. Your vote throughout the weeks ahead will therefore put more money in the pockets of more workers.*
>
> *Supporting the Tax Cuts and Jobs Act will ensure that those workers - those beneficiaries - are American.*
>
> *Sincerely,*
>
> *James C. Miller III, Former OMB Director, 1985-88*
>
> *Douglas Holtz-Eakin, American Action Forum (et. al.)*

As predicted, here is a short excerpt of quotes from some economists that oppose the GOP tax law:

> *"...If the U.S. enacts a tax bill similar to those currently moving through the House and Senate — and assuming no other changes in tax or spending policy — U.S. GDP will be substantially higher a decade from now than under the status quo"*
>
> *(Harvey, 2017)*
>
> *"...The second question asked whether passage of the Republican tax bills would mean "the US debt-to-GDP ratio will be substantially higher a decade from now than under the status quo." Here, too, the news was grim from Republicans. In this case, all but one economist agreed that the bills would blow up the deficit, and the out-lier, Stanford's Liran Einav, to have misread the question — he later clarified that he also agrees the bill would add to the debt.*
>
> *"How could it be otherwise?" asked MITs Daron Acemoglu. "Cut taxes. Lose money. Repeat," said Goolsbee. "This is at least is clear," said Yale's William Nordhaus: "No way the growth effects will be strong enough to offset the revenue losses." Even Darrell Duffie, the sole economist who agreed that the bill would boost GDP, says the plan will pile on debt.*
>
> *(Klein, 2017)*

The US is a high generator of income. Another defense to this argument is that the US economy, as of 2015, generated around 33 times the amount it borrowed, levels at which are argued to be sustainable (Carroll, 2015). However, generation of income may not be related necessarily to collections by the IRS, and hence may not be a reliable method to peg against net borrowings. Using the actual IRS collections may perhaps be a better measure of debt repayment ability.

Other criticisms leveled against the law are that corporations are not likely to invest this cash, as has been proven by history through time (CBPP, 2017). An estimate from the Tax Policy Center finds that about 70% of the benefits to corporate rate cuts through recent history ultimately flow to the top fifth (top 20%), and more than a third flows to the top 1%.

The counter is the trickle-down theory which holds that lowered corporate tax rates increase the 'trickle down' to workers whilst simultaneously increasing investments (thus more jobs).

Expert tips

There are far more changes to the law as regards to corporate taxes, but the main and most significant changes have been discussed herein. The main arguments that supporters make for reduction in corporate taxes are the trickle-down effect and increased investments by corporations. The arguments by the critics are that these decreases in corporate taxes are likely to increase the deficit, whilst subsequently taxing the rich at a lower rate than most people.

The US has been borrowing to meet the current budget deficits at a higher rate since the global financial crisis of 2007/8. A spurred economy, expected from TCJA, might serve to increase capital flow to the US, meaning that the government would not only borrow at a slower rate, but ultimately begin to collect more than it spends. At the end of the day, these are all hypothetical situations. TCJA is well-meaning, and sure, it might have ill-advised sections to it. As discussed, this is a very partisan law, and every side can make arguments in their favor.

PART II

Chapter 3 : Tax Rate Reform - Income Tax

Introduction to Tax Rate Reforms in terms of Income Tax

What is the law? A brief

Tax law in the US is constructed and implemented by the legislature, formed by your elected officials from various parts of the country. The IRS (Internal Revenue Service) is a federal agency with the specific mandate of enforcing these tax laws on the American people in the form of annual remittances of taxes as a percentage of income. However, the IRS is also charged with making tax related information available for those that may need assistance, as well as assisting anyone with concerns or issues with their taxes.

Income taxes are calculated on the basis of your income level, with the majority of individuals on the 'Pay-As-You-Go' system, meaning that income tax is paid on a pay check basis, with deductions made by the IRS on every individual pay check (US Tax Center - IRS, n.d.). It is also a gradual tax system, meaning that the more money you make, the more tax you pay. This is achieved through a system that has 7 marginal tax brackets for each filing status.

Individual Alternative Minimum Tax (AMT)

Alongside the regular income tax is the individual alternative minimum tax (AMT) that works in a similar manner to the old AMT law. It requires taxpayers to calculate their liabilities to the IRS twice, once would be under regular income tax bands and once under individual AMT (Tax and Policy Centre Briefing Book, 2016).

A taxpayer would then be required, if they fell under a specific category, to pay the higher amount of the two. Typically, though there are other characteristics that define those likely to pay, families with two children are 3 times as likely to pay the AMT, while those with three or more children are four times as likely to pay the AMT, all compared to those without children.

Due to the add-back of specific itemized deductions, many taxpayers were subject to pay AMT as the regular tax rate was lower than the AMT. However, because the new tax law eliminates miscellaneous itemized deductions whilst capping state deductions at $10,000, many of these taxpayers are no longer subject to the AMT. Additional provisions of the new tax law ensure that fewer people will be subjected to the AMT, reducing its overall relevance to the tax system.

Alimony

Alimony under TCJA is now non-deductible, thus cannot reduce the overall taxable income of the taxpayer, whilst those receiving the payments will not have the payment counted as additional income, thus increasing their taxable income. These were to the contrary with the old law.

What was the problem

Taxes, as they were instituted, were generally taxing the population at a higher rate, contrary to common economic theory that assumes that cuts on tax rates give higher economic incentive for people to work more, increasing the size of the economy from a productivity standpoint. Further, an argument to democracy is that wealth is generated through production, the fruits of which are money. One could therefore argue that it is the fundamental right of the producer to keep their wealth, except in the interest of giving a portion of it up in order to pay for public goods such as national defense and the justice system (Ozimek, 2017).

Other arguments for lower taxes are that private individuals and businesses are more efficient at spending than governments are, thus invalidating the need for the government to collect and inefficiently use more money, as that is likely to increase the amount that is wasted (Boaz, 2001). Another argument is that the foundation of the United States of America is based on smaller government, and because Congress is likely to spend money collected anyway, the only way to limit the reach and size of the government is to limit their financial power.

What does the new law do / require?

The new law specifies new tax brackets for different categories of tax payers. Tables 5 & 6 are breakdowns of the old tax brackets:

Old Singles Filing Rates

Singles	
Taxable Income	**Tax Rate**
$0 - $9,275	10% of taxable income
$9,276 - $37,650	$927.50 + 15% of the amount over $9,275
$37,651 - $91,150	$5,183.75 + 25% of the amount over $37,650
$91,151 - $190,150	$18,558.75 + 28% of the amount over $91,150
$190,151 - $ 413,350	$46,278.75 + 33% of the amount over $190,150
$413,351 - $415,050	$119,934.75 + 35% of the amount over $413,350
$415,051 or more	$120,529.75 + 39.6% of the amount over $415,050

Source: IRS

Married Filing Rates

Married Individuals Filing Jointly or Qualifying Widow(er)

Taxable Income	Tax Rate
$0 - $18,550	10% of taxable income
$18,551 - $75,300	$1,855 + 15% of the amount over $18,550
$75,301 - $151,900	$10,367.50 + 25% of the amount over $75,300
$151,901 - $231,450	$29,517.50 + 28% of the amount over $151,900
$231,451 - $413,350	$51,791.50 + 33% of the amount over $231,450
$413,351 - $466,950	$111,818.50 + 35% of the amount over $413,350
$466,951 or more	$130,578.50 + 39.6% of the amount over $466,950

Source: IRS

Married Filing Separately

Married Filing Separately

Taxable Income	Tax Rate
$0 - $9,275	10% of taxable income
$9,276 - $37,650	$927.50 + 15% of the amount over $9,275
$37,651 - $75,950	$5,183.75 + 25% of the amount over $37,650
$75,951 - $115,725	$14,758.75 + 28% of the amount over $75,950
$115,726 - $206,675	$25,895.75 + 33% of the amount over $115,725
$206,676 - $233,475	$55,909.25 + 35% of the amount over $206,675
$233,476 or more	$65,289.25 + 39.6% of the amount over $233,475

Source: IRS

Heads of Household

Taxable Income	Tax Rate
$0 - $13,250	10% of taxable income
$13,251 - $50,400	$1,325 + 15% of the amount over $13,250
$50,401 - $130,150	$6,897.50 + 25% of the amount over $50,400
$130,151 - $210,800	$26,835 + 28% of the amount over $130,150
$210,801 - $413,350	$49,417 + 33% of the amount over $210,800
$413,351 - $441,000	$116,258.50 + 35% of the amount over $413,350
$441,001 or more	$125,936 + 39.6% of the amount over $441,000

Source: IRS

The Jack & Jill Analogy (used in this book)

As is with the corporate tax rates, individual tax rates apply in brackets, with a standard amount paid, with a tax rate applied to amounts in excess of the lower end of the bracket (US Tax Center - IRS, n.d.).

This is best exemplified by Jack and Jill, a couple that decides to file their return together. Assuming that they, combined, earn $120,000, under the old tax law, the applicable tax would be a payment of $10,367.5 plus a 25% tax on the difference between the lower tax band amount ($75,300). The tax would therefore total to $ 120,000-$ 75,3000 = $ 44,700. A tax of 25% is then taxable on $ 44,700, amounting to $ 11,175. The total amount of regular tax paid by Jack and Jill is therefore $ 21,543. This is summarized below:

Jack & Jill example computation (old law)

Net income	$	120,000
Payable	$	10,367.5
Excess	$	44,700
Tax	$	11,175
Total tax	$	21,543

Source: computation

The Andreas Analogy (used in this book)

Andreas, a single man earning $ 60,000 a year would calculate his taxes as per the summary below:

Andreas example computation (old law)

Net income	**$**	**60,000**
Payable	$	5,183.75
Excess	$	22,350
Tax	$	5,588
Total tax	$	10,771

New Tax Brackets

The new tax brackets and rates for the same groups (shown previously) are as follows:

New Single Filing Rates

Singles	
Taxable Income	Tax Rate
$0 - $9,325	10% of taxable income
$9,326 - $37,950	$932.50 + 15% of the amount over $9,325
$37,951 - $91,900	$5,226.25 + 25% of the amount over $37,950
$91,901 - $191,650	$18,713.75 + 28% of the amount over $91,900
$191,651 - $416,700	$46,643.75 + 33% of the amount over $191,650
$416,701 - $418,400	$120,910.25 + 35% of the amount over $416,700
$418,401 or more	$121,505.25 + 39.6% of the amount over $418,400

New Married Filing Rates

Married Filing Jointly or Qualifying Widow(er)	
Taxable Income	Tax Rate
$0 - $18,650	10% of taxable income
$18,651 - $75,900	$1,865.00 + 15% of the amount over $18,650
$75,901 - $153,100	$10,452.50 + 25% of the amount over $75,900
$153,101 - $233,350	$29,752.50 + 28% of the amount over $153,100
$233,351 - $416,700	$52,222.50 + 33% of the amount over $233,350
$416,701 - $470,700	$112,728.00 + 35% of the amount over $416,700
$470,701 or more	$131,628.00 + 39.6% of the amount over $470,700

New `Head of Household` Filing Rates

Head of Household	
Taxable Income	**Tax Rate**
$0 - $13,350	10% of taxable income
$13,351 - $50,800	$1,335.00 + 15% of the amount over $13,350
$50,801 - $131,200	$6,952.50 + 25% of the amount over $50,800
$131,201 - $212,500	$27,052.50 + 28% of the amount over $131,200
$212,501 - $416,700	$49,816.50 + 33% of the amount over $212,500
$416,701 - $444,550	$117,202.50 + 35% of the amount over $416,700
$444,551 or more	$126,950.00 + 39.6% of the amount over $444,550

Source: IRS

New `Married-Filing Separately` Filing Rates

Married Filing Separately	
Taxable Income	**Tax Rate**
$0 - $9,325	10% of taxable income
$9,326 - $37,950	$932.50 + 15% of the amount over $9,325
$37,951 - $76,550	$5,226.25 + 25% of the amount over $37,950
$76,551 - $116,675	$14,876.25 + 28% of the amount over $76,550
$116,676 - $208,350	$26,111.25 + 33% of the amount over $116,675
$208,351 - $235,350	$56,364.00 + 35% of the amount over $208,350
$235,351 or more	$65,814.00 + 39.6% of the amount over $235,350

Source: IRS

Under the new tax law, Jack and Jill, as well as Andreas would pay taxes summarized below:

Jack & Jill example computation (new law)

Net income	$ 120,000
Payable	$ 10,452.5
Excess	$ 44,099
Tax	$ 11,025
Total tax	$ 21,477

Source: Computation

Andreas example computation (new law)

Net income	$ 60,000
Payable	$ 5,226.25
Excess	$ 22,049
Tax	$ 5,512
Total tax	$ 10,739

Source: Computation

What does this mean for Jack and Jill?

As per the analysis in the previous section, Jack and Jill's tax differences under the two laws is summarized below:

J&J tax comparison

J&J - Old			J&J - New		
Net income	$	120,000	Net income	$	120,000
Payable	$	10,367.5	Payable	$	10,452.5
Excess	$	44,700	Excess	$	44,099
Tax	$	11,175	Tax	$	11,025
Total tax	$	21,543	Total tax	$	21,477
Net tax savings				$ 65	

Source: Computation

Under the new tax law, J&J would benefit from a $ 65 tax saving for the year. This does not take into consideration any AMT tax considerations, but generally shows a reduction in their overall tax obligation under the new law.

...and Andreas

Andreas tax comparison

Andreas - Old		Andreas - New	
Net income	$ 60,000	Net income	$ 60,000
Payable	$ 5,183.75	Payable	$ 5,226.25
Excess	$ 22,350	Excess	$ 22,049
Tax	$ 5,588	Tax	$ 5,512
Total tax	$ 10,771	Total tax	$ 10,739
Net tax savings		$ 33	

Source: Computation

As is the case with J&J, Andreas will also see his tax obligation reduce by $ 33 per year. Again, these computations do not include AMT tax considerations but generally show a reduction in his overall tax obligation under the new law.

Misconceptions/ Criticisms/ Clarification

For one, the AMT was not repealed. However, because of the new law, fewer people will be subject to it. Further, because many people that were once required to pay AMT will not be considered going forwards, these individuals are likely to see significant reductions in their liabilities due to deductions that qualify under the regular tax law not being canceled out by the AMT.

One critique of the income tax law is that it is likely to benefit those that earn more by having a bigger reduction on their tax liability, meaning that they would save more money as a percentage of their income. Whilst this might be true, one must consider the overall reason why this might be so.

Reducing taxes on the most frequent tax bracket might cripple government's collections. Presenting breaks to those that are not as frequent might advance the government ideal of reduced taxes for the population whilst maintaining reasonable collections.

Another argument to be made about the changes to the alimony payment system, one which had been in place for a 75 year period, with one clear rule regarding alimony payments: that the payments were deductible for the payer, and the recipient would have to pay income tax on it. The removal of this understanding has arguably made the already complicated system of calculating alimony payments even more complex. For example, in California, judges and lawyers use certain software in order to calculate alimony. With the changes to the law, this renders the software obsolete, and throws an already complex process into disarray.

Individual health insurance mandate repealed

One of the requirements of the Affordable Care Act (ACA) is that individuals would face a penalty if they did not have a certain level of coverage. The new tax bill eliminates these penalties, making the choice of whether to be covered elective. This is likely to increase premiums for the ACA (Mitchell and Greenburg, 2018).

Expert tips

Readers should consider the effect of AMT on their tax obligations, especially those who have been paying it. The repeal of certain deductions on AMT are likely to reduce their overall tax obligation.

Those individuals going through or considering a divorce should seek advice on how the new tax law on alimony affects them. This will be crucial information in understanding the overall outcome, as well as the long-term effect your payments will have on your overall finances, on either side of the table.

"We can't afford to get divorced without that tax benefit, so we're going to stay together, and I don't mean happily."

- Ken Neumann, Center for Mediation and Training in New York City

PART III

Chapter 4 : Tax Benefits for Families and Individuals

TAX BENEFITS FOR FAMILIES AND INDIVIDUALS

What is the law? A brief

There is no specific tax law in the US that specifically addresses benefits per demographic such as families. However, in this section, we evaluate those laws that have been changed and are consequently likely to have an impact on taxes for those that pay taxes as families (or have family sizes that are directly impacted by the law.) Further, we will also focus on some of the impacts that the law has on individuals, although most of these impacts are likely to have been discussed in previous sections of this paper.

Some of the items that will be discussed in this section will include the increases in standard deduction, expansion of the Child Tax Credit (CTC), and the elimination of personal exemptions.

What was the problem

The tax benefits changes were brought in to benefit families. Arguably home owners were under some strain and that has now been removed. However, it is difficult to pin-point a specific challenge or problem that the law has improved for families. This is precisely due to the lack of specificity in addressing the various items that address the demographics in question.

What does the new law do / require?

Families

Perhaps, the largest change relates to the child tax credit determination. The TCJA features a number of shifts in amounts for dependents. The Mortgage Interest Deduction and Health Care penalty elimination will also affect families.

Child Tax Credit

The CTC, as part of the new TCJA law, has some significant changes, some of which include repealing exemptions for dependents. In order to compensate for this, the TCJA works to increase the child tax credit from $1,000 (fully refundable) to $2,000 ($1,400 of which is fully refundable).

Therefore, for joint filers with $400,000 income or less, and for individuals with $200,000 income or lower, these CTC cuts apply. The maximum age for the applicability of the CTC on families is children of age 16 and over (Clemens, 2018).

It should be noted, however, that once a child is 16 and dependent on their parents, the exemptions are replaced by a $500 non-refundable tax credit. This is likely to be of disadvantage when compared to the old law that had a $4,150 exemption deduction for those families with dependent children over the age of 16.

Mortgage Interest Deduction

The TCJA reduces from $1 million to 750,000 the loan limit for which a mortgage interest deduction claim for a mortgage taken out after 14 December 2017. The implications of this are that for those with homes valued at $750,000 or lower, a deduction on the interest on their homes can be taken on their taxes, easing the burden of purchasing and owning a home (Pickering, 2017).

Further, those loans applied for before 15 December 2017 and over $750,000 but under $1million will still be able to continue to claim home mortgage interest up to $1,000,000 as deductible. However, refinanced mortgages would have to have been approved before the cut-off date.

Health care penalties eliminated

Under the Affordable Care Act (ACA), American citizens are required to obtain healthcare as part of the individual mandate. This individual mandate requires the vast majority of Americans to purchase health insurance, thereby imposing penalties on those that choose not to, mostly those that are young and healthy, thereby deeming the purchase of premiums as unnecessary (Kliff, 2015). The aim of these penalties, which stood at $695 per person or 2% of household income (whichever is higher), was intended to force those individuals that did not deem the premiums necessary to take them up, thereby reducing overall premiums for all policy takers.

Individuals

As discussed, many of the individual benefits from the TCJA are discussed in earlier sections of this report. These include the lowering of income tax brackets and overall rates, as well as the repealing of the individual mandate. The TCJA is expected to impact the individual by increasing the economic potential of the U.S., thus benefiting them both directly (tax cuts) and more so, indirectly through better economic conditions that are likely to increase wages from both an absolute and 'real wages' (wages net of the impact of inflation) standpoint.

What does this mean for Jack and Jill?

The CTC means that taxpayers that don't owe tax but have a dependent under the age of 16 can claim a credit of up to $1,400, meaning that Jack and Jill are likely to benefit from the CTC if they have a child under the age of 16, allowing them larger net cash to them. Therefore, between the years 2018 to 2025, Jack and Jill will be able to access tax credits for each qualifying child. This means that if they have three children, they are due refunds of up to $1,400 per child ($4,200) annually, in addition to up to $600 per child in deductions ($1,800) annually. Though deductions do not necessarily translate directly to matching tax savings, they do go a long way to reducing the overall tax obligations for families, and thus increasing their liquidity.

Further, though interest rate deductions are likely to increase for those with homes valued at over $750,000, the law makes home ownership more equitable, with those earning enough to purchase a $750,000+ home being required to pay more in taxes for it due to lower levels of deductibles. One of the main driving forces behind this tax law was correction of perceived inequity, and although the law could have done more to address these issues, it has attempted to correct these with such changes.

Finally, the elimination of the ACA's individual mandate means that households are able to choose whether or not to access healthcare.

...and Andreas

This applies for Jack and Jill, as well as Andreas, as an elimination of the penalty adds cash back to them if they choose to do away with premium payments.

Expert tips

It would benefit families to take advantage of the higher tax deductibles on CTCs, especially since they expire at the end of 2025. These higher deductibles are likely to have a real impact on the cash available to families.

Young individuals with healthy lifestyles can also evaluate the benefits of opting out of the ACA and use premium payments as a means of increasing liquidity and investments overall. At the minimum, the $695 increase in cash is over the next 8 years is likely to benefit from investment growth.

PART IV

Chapter 5 : Education

EDUCATION

What is the law? A brief

The laws around the education sector are centered around, and naturally so, those that are saving for their college education, or those paying off the debts associated with education. There are several laws that are directly associated with education.

What was the problem

The point of building a tax code around the education sector is due to the association of a moral and intelligent society with its level of education. Therefore, in order to build a society with appropriate skills for its own furtherance, education is a key determinant.

It then follows that those policies should work in order to build the current education system. The Harvard Business Review's analysis on the current state of the education system seems to be underwhelming, with the US system scoring far below the leaders in math and reading, with 74% of 12th graders scoring 'below proficient' in math and 62% in reading (Carmichael, 2012).

Further, the percentage of jobs needing a college degree is increasing relative to the entire population, and thus policies put in place by government would be well placed if they are to serve to improve the education system.

What does the new law do / require?

The American opportunity credit AOC remains unchanged

The American opportunity credit (AOC) of up to $2,500 per eligible student, $1,000 of which may be refundable. The law is applicable to each student for 4 tax years, and only if the student in question has not completed the first 4 years of post-secondary education before the end of the tax year. This is intended to encourage college or university enrollment within a specified time range (4 years), with the intention of making the transition between high school and university smooth, thereby increasing the likelihood of graduation. Given the aforementioned requirement for better skilled workers in the U.S., the retention of the AOC plays its part in ensuring that parents (those that can afford it) and students are incentivised to ensure education is completed to at least the university level.

Changes to the 529 savings accounts

A 529 plan is a savings plan with tax advantages afforded in order to encourage saving for future college costs. Also, legally known as 'qualified tuition plans', these 529 plans are sponsored by states, state agencies or education institutions. They are also authorized by section 529 of the Internal Revenue Code, hence the referral as 529 plans (U.S. Securities and Exchange Commission - Investor Publications, 2017).

Contributions to these plans are not tax deductible in nature, but those funds deposited for such initiatives are not taxed on their growth, and can grow tax free until distributed. The TCJA expanded the usage of the 529 plans to include elementary and secondary school tuitions, qualifying under religious, private and public schools.

Many education benefits stay in place

In addition to the AOC, many other education incentives and breaks remain static, some of which include the lifetime learning credit, non-taxable scholarship and grant rules, as well as the education savings bond exclusion.

What does this mean for Jack and Jill?

J&J's family, consisting of 3 children that qualify for the AOC, would receive up to $3,000 in refundable taxes, depending on the tax qualifications they possess. It would be best advised that one consults a tax advisor for further clarification on the same. They would also qualify for the additional $2,500 tax deductible on the AOC (remaining from the $1,000 refundable credit), reducing the overall tax obligation on the family. Further, if they have a 529 account and are able to invest money by saving it for future higher education spending, they would not need to pay federal taxes on their investment gains, thereby acting as both an investment and savings plan at once (Pickering, 2017).

...and Andreas

Individuals like Andreas are likely to be struggling with a student loan, and for him, it does not mean much in the way of change. However, things staying the same beats them turning worse, and the $2,500 student loan interest deduction on the overall taxable income is one way of lowering his tax burden. It should be noted that student loan deduction has an income-based phase out, meaning that there is a slight risk that a small percentage of people may not qualify due to this. Taxpayers that refinance their student loans are eligible to continue claiming the deduction as part of their tax deduction calculations.

In some circumstances, the TCJA has left mechanisms in place for student loan repayment assistance tax-free if these payments are made on behalf of taxpayers. These payments are non-taxable if they are received under following:-

- A state education loan repayment program

- The National Health Service Corps (NHSC) loan repayment program

- Any other state loan repayment or loan forgiveness program

Misconceptions/ Criticisms/ Clarification

Some studies have shown that the already well to do may benefit from the 529 plans as they allow them significant tax breaks, especially considering data that suggests that in 2010, parents with 529 accounts had around three times the median income of those that didn't (Lobosco, 2017).

The premise is that only those families who have the capability of saving would be able to enroll for such a program, and there is a large portion of the population that is simply unable to save.

The flip-side, however, is that 529 plans may motivate those with suspect spending habits to save for future education. Further, the ability to currently use 529 plans for elementary and secondary schools means that children may be able to access quality education in their earlier and formative years rather than later, thereby increasing their chances of completing their higher studies.

Expert tips

Investing in a 529 plan will likely impact on a student's eligibility to receive financial aid on a needs basis. However, for many families, the savings held in 529 accounts constitute largely of loans from financial institutions.

It would therefore be beneficial to both the parents and students to ensure that optimal levels of savings are put aside. This will ensure that a lower proportion of debt is required in order to pay for higher learning (Burkett & Burkett, 2018). Tuition for elementary and secondary schools qualifying under 'qualified higher education expense' under the 529 plans means that the TCJA now enables parents to pay for elementary and secondary schools of their choice. This is limited to $10,000 for elementary and secondary (when combined) per single beneficiary, and includes expenses for tuition in connection with enrollment or attendance at any school elementary and upwards, including religious, private or public schools.

PART V

Chapter 6 : Deductions and Exclusions

DEDUCTIONS AND EXCLUSIONS

What is the law? A brief

There is no single overriding law that specifies all the deductions and exclusions provided for by the TCJA. As a result, many of the deductions and exclusions discussed in earlier sections of this text are likely to overlap into this section.

However, we will dive a little deeper into some of the specific deductions and exclusions that are likely to matter to you, as well as 'compiling' them so as to give you a rounded and objective view of the major sections and changes provided by the TCJA.

What was the problem

Deductions are typically aimed at encouraging positive externalities. There may not have been a single issue with the outgoing law per se, but there were a few arguments against it, specifically those that argue against the role of the government in as far as the economy is concerned. Proponents of small government argue that the government is not as efficient with spending as the private sector (Boaz, 2001). Further, the general pro-tax cuts argument is that tax cuts are likely to make working today more attractive than it is tomorrow, if these cuts are temporary.

Therefore, this is likely to lead to higher aggregate supply to the labour force, which is likely to increase overall productive output (Thoma, 2009). It should also be noted that Congress is notorious for spending each and every dollar that they can afford themselves, which goes against sound financial principles that revolve around preservation and savings, all the while making critically assessed spending and investment decisions. With government, bureaucracy and socialist principles put the perceived needs of the people ahead of these principles, thus likely to lead to inefficient and unnecessary spending.

What does the new law do / require?

Individual tax provisions

The TCJA retains the 7 tax brackets but reduces the overall tax rates, with the top marginal federal tax rate dropping from 39.6% to 37% for high income individuals. The new tax general income tax rates for the 7 brackets mentioned are 10%, 12%, 22%, 24%, 32%, 35% and 37%. One is best advised to consult a tax professional that is likely to interpret these, especially since standard deductions are likely to reduce the overall taxable income, thereby reducing the overall tax obligation (Hamilton Tharp LLP, 2017).

Personal exemption deductions have been eliminated under TCJA, meaning that personal deductions of $4,150 applicable in the outgoing law is now eliminated. This is applicable for the years 2018-2025, with Congress likely to decide on whether to continue with the old law or to keep the new one.

Standard deductions have increased. For the tax years between 2018 - 2025, standard deductions have increased to $12,000 for individuals (previously $6,500), $18,000 for head of household filers ($9,550), $24,000 for married individuals filing a joint return ($13,000). Most of these deductions have increased by close to 100% (Hamilton Tharp LLP, 2017).

Medical expense deduction limit reduced for the tax period between 2017-2018, from 10% of annual gross income (AGI) to 7.5% of AGI for all taxpayers.

TCJA also eliminates the 'Pease' limitation on itemized deductions. Under the outgoing law, itemized deductions were limited whilst under the TCJA, all limitations have been eliminated. This means that should an individual's itemized deductions exceed their standard deduction, the individual is free to deduct all expenses that qualify for deduction without necessarily having to use a limit on the overall deduction amount (Hamilton Tharp LLP, 2017)

Other tax provisions

Corporate taxes have been reduced from a rate of 37% to 21%. Further, corporate AMT was repealed for tax years after 2017, meaning that corporations are able to use standard deductions, over and above the rate deductions, to lower their overall tax bills.

What does this mean for Jack and Jill?

A reduction in the standard deduction rate means that the overall tax obligation for individuals is likely to reduce, as highlighted as part of the dedicated income tax section of the paper. Married couples like J&J, as well as singles such as Andreas are all likely to benefit from the higher standard deduction amounts in the TCJA.

The reduction in the percentage of deductible medical expenses is likely to reduce the impact of medical expenses deductions, thus slightly raising tax dues to the IRS for this specific category. However, this applies only to medical expenses which are far more sporadic than income taxes, and thus unlikely to have as big an impact.

A reduction in the overall corporate tax rate, and the repeal of the AMT mean that businesses are likely to increase their overall spending on investments and employee welfare.

...and Andreas

Andreas would likely benefit directly as an employee from reduced income tax rates, in addition to the likely economic stimulus from additional investments made by companies due to lower tax rates. J&J are likely to increase their revenues due to lowered taxes on pass through entities. Changes to the CTC are also likely to improve liquidity should their children qualify. Further, the elimination on limits of itemized deductions is also likely to reduce their overall tax obligation due to lowered taxable income from increased amounts of deductions.

Misconceptions/ Criticisms/ Clarification

A critique of the itemized deduction is that it is most likely to benefit those that are already wealthy. Reasons for this are that those individuals with deductions that outpaced the already increased standard deduction are likely to be categorized as high earners. Therefore, in as far as perceived equity is concerned, this particular section of the law is likely to benefit those from wealthier sections of the American society. Given that the TCJA was billed as one in which issues such as disparity of incomes would be addressed, there is a direct contravention by including this in the law.

However, it should be noted that laws are a result of bi-partisan negotiations, most likely some parts of the law have to be tweaked to ensure all interested parties are catered to.

Expert tips

Provisions to the state and local tax deduction are limited to a rule stating that an individual may not claim an itemized deduction in 2017 on a per-payment of income tax for a future tax year in order to avoid the dollar limitation applicable for tax years beginning after 2017. This means that one cannot take advantage of current rates and apply them to future obligations. Should the rate therefore vary in the future, it is critical to ensure that one knows this (Hamilton Tharp LLP, 2017).

PART VI

Chapter 7 : Increase in Estate and Gift Tax Exemption

INCREASE IN ESTATE AND GIFT TAX EXEMPTION

What is the law? A brief

The TCJA brought with it changes to the wealth transfer tax system (WTTS). These are laws that prescribe the federal taxes on transference of properties freely given, such as a bequest or a gift from a donor. There are 3 types of federal wealth transfer taxes, the estate tax, the gift tax and the generation-skipping tax (Graham & Dunn, 2011). In addition to these, many states have their own requirements for the treatment of inheritance or estate tax. The estate tax (the gift and generation-skipping taxes build on the foundations of the estate tax), is also referred to as the death tax (Premack, 2017).

The federal estate tax is imposed on all taxes owned by deceased person. The value of the assets is based on fair market value, with value assigned. All the assets owned by a decedent are subject to this tax, including all of those taxes that the individual had an interest in. An example of assets that might qualify include a trust in which the deceased had determined who to bequeath an estate. All the assets included in this trust would be subject to this tax (Graham & Dunn, 2011).

The federal gift tax is one that is intended to deter evasion of the estate tax, a process in which a decedent could simply give away their properties during their lifetime as opposed to doing so near or at their death.

The federal generation-skipping tax is intended to avoid even further instances of tax evasion on gift and estate taxes, some of which include instances in which an individual may give his children his assets in trust for life, with the balance of those assets to their children (decedents grandchildren) at their death. Given that the children did not have any 'incidents of ownership' in those assets, said assets under regular gift tax laws could pass from the children to the grandchildren free of estate taxes.

What was the problem

The law here aimed to simplify the regime with regards to gifts. There wasn't a specific issue with the outgoing law. The associated changes to the law relate more in the amounts exempted in as far as the transference of wealth is concerned.

What does the new law do / require?

The new version of the estate tax is significant in its changes. As of 2017, an individual had the ability to pass on $5.49 million in assets without being subject to federal estate tax. For married individuals, this amount is doubled to $10.98 million. These exemptions are due to increase in 2018 to $5.6 million for individuals and $11.2 million for married couples (Corporate Direct, 2017). Considering that as of the year 2000 the exemption was $1 million, the exemptions have certainly grown over the years.

Gift taxes are assessed annually and not necessarily at death. As of 2017, the gift tax exemption for 2018 stands at $15,000, meaning that an individual can gift that amount to anyone without notifying the IRS.

What does this mean for Jack and Jill?

J&J, if they be so fortunate, can bequeath an estate of up to $11.2 million to their children without having to pay the estate tax. In addition to this, they would also be able to gift their children and grandchildren to the tune of $15,000 each, with no limit to the number of legitimate individuals that qualify. For example, if the two have 10 grandchildren, the gift tax exemption would allow them to each gift $15,000 to each of their grandchildren, meaning that it would work out to $15,000*2*10 = $300,000 that would be transferred to them (Corporate Direct, 2017). . The significant size of the exemptions means that there is little value for an individual who does not need to transfer much more or within the exemption amounts, as they could do this with the estate tax for free.

Misconceptions/ Criticisms/ Clarification

It would sound that most of our critiques are related to equity, but this underscores some of the pledges that the GOP made to the country when drafting and campaigning for the law when it was in bill format. The TCJA can be argued to be favoring the rich and increasing inequality. As put by Senator Chuck Grassley of Iowa, however,

"An estate tax effectively and unfairly taxes a person's earnings twice: first when they earn it and again when they die. And, he added, it penalizes savers without touching spenders.

"I think not having the estate tax recognizes the people that are investing, as opposed to those that are just spending every darn penny they have, whether it's on booze or women or movies"

(Krieg, 2017)

Though colorful, Grassley makes a fair point. Though the tax does favor the wealthy, they should be allowed equal rights as prescribed by the constitution. In addition, though the country would certainly be better off when consumption and spending go up, investments take a more long-term approach, ensuring that the interests of the country's economy are sustainable.

A free country must recognize that wealth is created through production, and that the owner of that production shall be entitled to its benefits, and therefore its wealth.

Expert tips

Families with assets bases that are significantly higher than exemption amounts per year can reduce their tax obligations, albeit perhaps only modestly rather than largely, by using the gift tax exemption and spreading the number of people that they gift these amounts to (one would assume family). Over a long period of time, and combined with the estate exemptions, the taxes avoided (and not evaded, which is illegal) using this method might just be substantial in amount.

PART VII

Chapter 8 : Extension of Time Limit for contesting IRS Levy

EXTENSION OF TIME LIMIT FOR CONTESTING IRS LEVY

What is the law? A brief

An IRS levy arises when the IRS is legally required to notify you the first time it collects or has the intention to collect a tax liability by taking your property or the rights to that property. Further, if the IRS intends to attach said levy on your bank accounts, you will receive a 'Final Notice of Intent to Levy and Notice of Your Right to a Hearing', also referred to as a levy notice. The IRS has the power to determine tax and perform collections on these taxes, power conferred to it by the federal government (Hartsock, 2013).

Once you receive the levy, you generally have to respond within 30 days, and the letter (the one with the levy notice) is likely to have the letters 'LT 11' or 'LT 1058' on it. It would be in your interest to appeal the process within the 30 days as it allows you a few options on how to work out the situation. For one, an appeal will allow you to pursue options whilst the process is halted. Once an appeal is lodged with the IRS, you are entitled to a 9-month period in which you are required to bring forward a civil suit. If anything, taking advantage of the appeal works to give more time (Tax Debt Help, 2017). The new law addresses the extension of the amount of time an appellate window must be in force before the IRS can claim the property and the amount of time in which the IRS must repay for assets sold unduly or incorrectly.

The second reason it would be valuable to appeal the process is that it is particularly difficult to get any of your property back once it is seized by the IRS. This is so because the IRS, once it places a levy on your assets, adds a deficit to its books and will work to recover the same in order to balance the books.

What was the problem

There was a perception that the original time limits were too short. The length with which you had to bring forth a civil suit was 9 months after the appeal process. Similarly, the amount of time with which the IRS had to pay back/ return assets seized wrongly was 9 months.

What does the new law do / require?

The new law extends the periods discussed above to 2 years for both parties. This means that the IRS has a longer amount of time before they are required to return wrongly seized assets, whilst the tax payer can take longer to bring forth a civil case against the levy, but only if the appeal is lodged in time. It is therefore in your best interests to ensure that the appeal is lodged quickly.

What does this mean for Jack and Jill Enterprises? (and Andreas Coffee Shop as well)

This only applies to Jack, Jill or Andreas if they have a tax obligation that the IRS intends to collect on. Once they receive the initial notice, they should consider their options. A great way to start is by familiarizing themselves with the process, consulting professionals on the same, and then commencing the appeals process.

Misconceptions/ Criticisms/ Clarification

An individual who wishes to appeal the process would be required to follow either the collection due process (CPD) or the collections appeal program (CAP). The CDP is available to those who receive the following notices:

- Notice of Federal Tax Lien Filing and Your Right to a Hearing, under IRC 6320

- Final Notice – Notice of Intent to Levy and Notice of Your Right to a Hearing

- Notice of Jeopardy Levy and Right of Appeal

- Notice of Levy on Your State Tax Refund – Notice of Your Right to a Hearing

- Post Levy Collection Due Process (CDP) Notice

The CAP program is available for the following actions:

- Before or after the IRS files a Notice of Federal Tax Lien

- Before or after the IRS levies or seizes your property

- Termination, or proposed termination, of an installment agreement

- Rejection of an installment agreement

- Modification, or propose modification of an installment agreement

Generally, CAP results in a faster appeals decision and is applicable to a broader range of collection actions (IRS, n.d.).

It is important to note that, with respect to installment agreements, the IRS cannot issue a levy until 30 days from the rejection or termination of said installment agreement. Therefore, should you lodge an appeal on the levy in 30 days from the rejection or termination, the IRS cannot issue a levy on your assets until the appellate process is complete (Shamoun, 2013).

Expert tips

The following are tips on when to consider appealing a tax levy:

- You have paid your taxes in full. A situation that may arise with the IRS failing to record your payment. You should start the appeals process in the interest of protecting your assets.

- You are making payments as part of an installment agreement. If the payments are timely, you would be considered to be in the IRS's good books.

- You have already applied for and submitted an offer in compromise. An offer in compromise is an IRS program that allows you to make them an offer that is lower than the total amount you owe. The IRS may accept your offer and wipe the rest of the debt. You will be in good standing with the IRS and you will need to be in compliance for 5 years going forward (Tax Debt Help, 2017).

- You receive an incorrect levy notice by accident.

- You are filing for bankruptcy, which puts a halt on all collection activities, including tax debt collections. If the IRS sends the notice of intent to levy during your bankruptcy proceedings, then the levy should be voided. Do contact your attorney or tax consultant for more advice.

- The IRS made a procedural error. The IRS must follow a strict procedural process before issuing a tax levy, so if they made an error you can appeal. The procedure must include the IRS assessing your liability and sending a notice to demand payment. If they can then prove that you neglected or refused to pay the amount, the IRS will then send you a final notice of intent to levy and give you 30 days to appeal.

- The statute of limitation, which is usually 10 years for collection by the IRS, has expired. The IRS has no right to levy on you if the amount concerned was accrued more than 10 years ago.

- Your spouse (or ex-spouse) bears responsibility for the debt, and you can prove that you are not liable for it.

- You may prefer alternative collection options such as settlement or payment plans (Tax Debt Help, 2017).

PART VIII

Chapter 9 : Deduction for Qualified Business Income of Pass-Through Entities

DEDUCTION FOR QUALIFIED BUSINESS IN-COME OF PASS – THROUGH ENTITIES

What is the law? A brief

Pass-through companies are those that are characterized by their incomes 'passing through' directly to the owners of the businesses, thus treating said income as income tax rather than corporation taxes. Most American business are of this nature, with some 95% of the total number of businesses classified under this category (Krupkin & Looney, 2017). Such types of businesses include sole proprietorships, S-corporations and partnerships.

Due to their scale in number, along with the fact that they earn a majority of U.S. business income, operate across a variety of industries thus having an economy-wide impact, they are affected by both corporate and individual tax systems. The nature of these businesses and the impact that they have on the economy makes legislation on their taxes a complicated topic, a topic of which has led to a lot of discussion and debate.

In short, therefore, taxes for pass though businesses that qualify as pass-through entities have their income passed to their owners. The owner of the businesses is then subject to the taxes that he or she qualifies for as stipulated under the tax brackets that he or she falls under. AMT taxes may apply for those individuals with significant deductibles on their regular tax computation.

What was the problem

At the federal level, these types of businesses have historically been taxed at a top marginal tax rate of 44.6%. Adding state-level taxes to this rate means that many businesses in the US have top marginal tax rates that exceed 47%. Considering that the influence of pass-through businesses has grown in the US over time since the 80s to its current level, it would seem that, on the face of it, that these taxes have not had a significant impact on the emergence and growth of such businesses. What this means is that, despite the high tax rates some of these companies have to pay, the overall effect appears to be minimal, especially when considering the growth in influence that pass-through entities have on the overall economy.

However, given the new tax corporate tax rates passed into law, it would have been incredibly short-sighted to reduce the corporate tax rate from 35% to 21%, all the while remaining static on pass-through businesses, especially considering that these businesses account for 95% of the total number of businesses in America (Greenburg, 2017). President Trump, in his commitment to lowering of taxes, made it clear that all Americans would benefit from the then proposed tax bill, and therefore, to exclude 95% of all businesses from those that benefit would have been not only unpopular, but unfair. It should also be noted that the majority of pass-through businesses are taxed at the top individual tax rates.

It should also be considered that pass-through businesses, as of 2011, employed more than 50% of the private sector work force, as well as 37% of the total private sector payroll (Pomerleau, 2015). The very essence Trump's tax plan is to spur growth by reducing organizational cost, thus freeing up cash for these businesses to utilize by spending on worker's welfare, investing in the expansion of the business, or both. Therefore, it would have been negligent for the then bill to propose significant tax reductions on C-corporations without passing these benefits to pass-through businesses as well, as this would likely go against the very reasons the tax cuts were proposed in the first place.

In the new law, businesses/corporations will pay less taxes due to a reduction on their top rate from 35% to 20%. This is done as part of the amendments to Sec. 11011 – Deduction for Qualified Business Income – of the 1986 Internal Revenue Code (Tax and Job Cuts Act of 2017).

What does the new law do / require?

The new tax rates on pass-through income specifies that, for those businesses making a profit in any given year, certain businesses qualify for a 20% pass-through deduction on their business. Some service-specific industries, such as law, professional services and health, are excluded from those that would benefit from such, except from joint filers with income below $315,000, and other filers with income below $157,500, are able to claim the deduction (Fontinelle, 2018). In addition, businesses that exceed this earnings threshold will see their deduction limited to the higher of 50% of total wages they pay or 25% of total wages paid plus 2.5% of tangible depreciable property at cost.

While these pass-through businesses may not necessarily benefit from a tax cut as significant as the ones made to the corporate tax rate, it is still important to note that they do receive the tax rate. The GOP argument to made in favor of reducing the pass-through income tax by granting these tax cuts are that these businesses will be motivated to reduce their overall tax liabilities by taking advantage of the deductions by way of deducting 50% of total wages paid out to employees. This would then mean that employees would receive higher earnings, and that this would therefore lead to higher spend on the economy by those that form the largest base by population size. In addition to this, reduction of overall taxes for pass-through businesses means that these taxpayers would be taxed at lower tax rates, freeing up capital that they can use for capital expenditure. Further laws in the tax plan also encourage the uptake of capital assets by granting taxpayers tax incentives to do so.

What does this mean for Jack and Jill Enterprises? (and Andreas Coffee Shop as well)

Tax through computations are complex, especially considering the deductibles that will form part of the allowable 20% deduction from the TCJA. For the sake of simple computation, let us consider J&J from the income tax section. We will also assume that they can take advantage of the entire 20% deductible. A 20% deductible on the business' $120,000 income means that their taxable income would reduce by $24,000 (20% * $120, 000.) Therefore, their taxable income would fall to $96,000.

Singles tax tables under TCJA

Singles	
Taxable Income	**Tax Rate**
$0 - $9,325	10% of taxable income
$9,326 - $37,950	$932.50 + 15% of the amount over $9,325
$37,951 - $91,900	$5,226.25 + 25% of the amount over $37,950
$91,901 - $191,650	$18,713.75 + 28% of the amount over $91,900
$191,651 - $416,700	$46,643.75 + 33% of the amount over $191,650
$416,701 - $418,400	$120,910.25 + 35% of the amount over $416,700
$418,401 or more	$121,505.25 + 39.6% of the amount over $418,400

Source: Forbes

Married tax tables under TCJA

Married Filing Jointly or Qualifying Widow(er)	
Taxable Income	**Tax Rate**
$0 - $18,650	10% of taxable income
$18,651 - $75,900	$1,865.00 + 15% of the amount over $18,650
$75,901 - $153,100	$10,452.50 + 25% of the amount over $75,900
$153,101 - $233,350	$29,752.50 + 28% of the amount over $153,100
$233,351 - $416,700	$52,222.50 + 33% of the amount over $233,350
$416,701 - $470,700	$112,728.00 + 35% of the amount over $416,700
$470,701 or more	$131,628.00 + 39.6% of the amount over $470,700

Source: Forbes

Therefore, J&J would then compute their tax obligation as per the schedule below:

Computation of J&J as a pass-through

Net income	$	96,000
Payable	$	10,452.5
Excess	$	20,099
Tax	$	5,025
Total tax	$	15,477

Source: computation

A side-by-side comparison of the J&J as an individual against pass-through is summarized in the table below:

Computation of J&J - individual vs pass-through					
J&J - Old			**J&J - New**		
Net income	$	120,000	Net income	$	96,000
Payable	$	10,452.5	Payable	$	10,452.5
Excess	$	44,099	Excess	$	20,099
Tax	$	11,025	Tax	$	5,025
Total tax	$	21,477	Total tax	$	15,477
Net tax savings			$ 6,000		

Source: computation

Under the new deduction, J&J would receive a net reduction in their tax obligation amounting to $ 6,000. This does not exclude any potential benefits from investment expenditure.

Misconceptions/ Criticisms/ Clarification

These benefits will expire in 2025. Unless the U.S. Congress decides to extend the lowered tax benefits beyond its term (and it would be in a position to do so), then these benefits are short-term and will only be in effect for a period of 8 years.

Total revenue collection will reduce by $289 billion on pass-through businesses alone. This would add to the federal deficit that the U.S. is currently having to contend with, thus going against the very purpose of the tax bill to begin with. However, should the economy rebound and grow as a result of this, the proponents of this bill argue that the net effect will be an increase in collections by the government.

Expert tips

Due to the restructuring of this pass-through business tax law, as well as the corporate tax law, businesses that qualify will be able to write-off 100% of the cost of capital expenses from 2018 for 5 years. This means that, instead of writing-off these expenses gradually over time, businesses can significantly reduce their tax obligation if they invest in capital-related investments.

Employees may also consider setting up themselves as contractors or consultants in order to reduce their overall tax obligations. However, those doing so will have to consider the added employer responsibilities they would be taking on for Medicare and Social Security taxes, as well as those taxes associated with their own health insurance and other benefits.

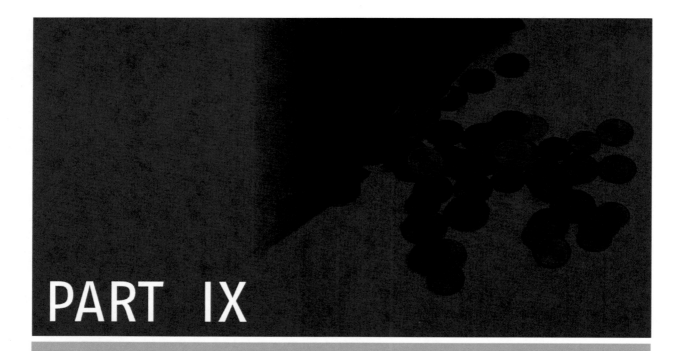

PART IX

Chapter 10 : Business Losses and Net Operating Losses (NOLS) for Corporate and Non-Corporate Taxpayers.

BUSINESS LOSSES AND NET OPERATING LOSSES (NOLS) FOR CORPORATE AND NON-CORPORATE TAXPAYERS

What is the law? A brief

A net operating loss arises from a situation in which a business incurs higher costs at an operation level than the revenue it generates, meaning that the business is unable to fund its operations using internally generated funds. The laws around the treatment of losses (financially) is one that prescribes how businesses shall account for these losses as part of their financial reporting, and the involves the allowable treatment and limitations of losses by businesses.

What was the problem

Again, in a similar fashion to the sections that came before this one, there was not a single specific issue with the preceding law, only that changes have been made under TCJA. Some of the changes involved include how businesses treat taxes incurred before the new law, for how many years, as well as any changes that might have been instituted as part of the new law.

What does the new law do / require?

Limitations for post-2017 losses for corporations.

Tax years beginning 2018 are modified by the TCJA to ensure that corporations can only use their NOL carry over to offset 80% of their net taxable income. Further, the new laws governing NOLs stipulate that these carry forwards are valid indefinitely, as opposed to the 20-year limit that was imposed by the previous law. However, those losses that were incurred before 2018 remain the same. This means that these losses can be carried back two years and forward 20 years, with no taxable limit to using pre-2018 losses.

The TCJA also sets limits on the carry back of losses. Carry back of losses means that losses incurred in one year can be used to offset profits in the year before that, meaning that a business could use the carry back to reduce profits, thereby reducing tax liabilities. Those companies that would have already paid these taxes can apply for credits to their taxes that can be carried forward, because the business will have paid excess taxes in the year in which the carry back was performed.

Business losses limitation on non-corporate taxpayers.

The new law specifies a limit on the treatment of business losses, specifically, the use of such losses by non-corporate taxpayers. As part of the outgoing law, losses incurred as part of a fully-fledged business could be used to offset those incomes that are not related to the business (non-business income; may include dividends, interest and capital gains), with no limit to the extent with which said loss may impact the overall tax obligation by the filer. Beginning 2018 to 2025, taxpayers are limited to a $500,000 deduction (for married filing jointly taxpayers) of such losses on non-business income. All amounts above this limit are considered "excess business losses" and are thus carried forward. These excess losses will also be treated as part of the taxpayers overall NOL carry forward, meaning that in subsequent taxable years, the carry forwards will be subjected to the new 80% NOL limits (Dillon & Hobbs, 2018).

What does this mean for Jack and Jill Enterprises? (and Andreas Coffee Shop as well)

J&J have a decent sized business. For the sake of calculation (example), let us assume that they earn an NOL for the year 2018 amounting to $850,000. Below is a comparison of the outcomes for the business under the tax law before and after TCJA:

Comparison of 2017 and 2018 loss effects

J&J Business	2017	2018
Taxable income	$ 750,000	$ 750,000
J&J NOL	$ 850,000	$ 850,000
Taxable income limit	No limit	80%
Tax deduction amount	$ 850,000	$ 680,000
Tax due	$ -100,000	$ 70,000
Treatment	Carry forward to 2018	Pay $ 70,000 in taxes

Source: computation

The new TCJA law on NOLs is tougher on businesses that attract losses. A business, under the old law, would have been able to deduct their entire loss from taxable income due to the lack of a limit that guides the extent of the deduction. However, given the fact that the new law only allows for an 80% deduction of the NOL on taxable income, an $850,000 loss incurred in 2017, as an example (does not consider any external factors that may influence these computations), would lead to a $100,000 carry forward to taxes in 2018. However, if the same loss is incurred in 2018, assuming that there is no carry forward from 2017, the net effect would be that the same business by J&J would owe $ 70,000 to the federal government.

The next table analyses a similar situation for J&J, but assumes that the $100,000 was carried forward from 2017. This example calculation aims to show how these losses would be treated in 2018 for losses incurred in the previous tax regime:

Effect of tax as per old regime

J&J Business	2017
Taxable income	$ 750,000
J&J NOL	$ 850,000
Taxable income limit	No limit
Tax deduction amount	$ 850,000
Tax due	$ -100,000
Treatment	Carry forward to 2018

Source: computation

The tax liability computations for 2017 remain valid as the new law does not interfere with these. Therefore, the $ 100,000 liability is carried forward to the following year, and is valid for carry forwards for the 20 years thereafter.

Effect of tax as per new regime

J&J Business	2018
Taxable income	$ 750,000
J&J NOL	$ 850,000
Taxable income limit	80%
Tax deduction amount	$ 680,000
Tax liability	$ 70,000
Carried forward from 2017	$ -100,000
Tax due	$ -30,000
Treatment	Tax credit of $ 30,000 carried forward to 2019

Source: computation

The new tax regime, as discussed, allows for carry forwards for those years preceding 2018, as did the old law. Therefore, the $ 100,000 tax credit from 2017 would be carried forward to 2018. This amount is then deducted from the tax liability that is calculated independently, thus arriving at a $ 30,000 tax credit that is then carried forward to 2019.

Misconceptions/ Criticisms/ Clarification

Calculation of excess business losses are performed by aggregating income and deductions from all of the trades or businesses that a taxpayer operates. This also extends to couples that file joint returns. Therefore, if a husband and wife have separate business but file a joint return, a $500,000 limit to their excess business loss applies to their entire aggregated income and deductions, and thus cannot be used to only offset one spouse's income. Essentially, those filing a joint return must aggregate their income and deductions.

Married couples that incur non-corporate business losses to one of them would be served by informing themselves of the provisions of this section of the TCJA.

Business losses for a non-corporate taxpayer within a tax can be used to offset the losses of one spouse by applying these losses to the other spouse's non-business income. This would mean that the non-business income (and by extension, the net taxable income) would be reduced by the amount of the excess business loss.

However, it should be noted that a non-corporate taxpayer can only offset a maximum of $250,000 as individual (filing separately) and $500,000 for married individuals (filing jointly).

PART X

Chapter 11: Elimination of the Section 199 Deduction

Elimination of the Section 199 Deduction

What is the law? A brief

The section 199 deduction is also known as the "domestic production activities deduction" (DPAD) and is geared primarily towards the manufacturing sector, although it has application in other sectors that shall be discussed later on. The basis of the act was that it was created as part of the American Jobs Creation Act of 2004 in order to incentivise companies engaged in specific activities with the aim of keeping and/ or creating jobs within the U.S. (KPMG, 2015).

This section of the law intends to achieve this by easing the tax burden of those companies involved in domestic manufacturing, thus making those facilities more advantageous against those players in the global market place. The law can also be used by those organizations that are involved in the manufacture, production, extraction or growth of tangible property by the taxpayer, including all tangible personal property (with the exception of land and buildings), as well as computer software and sound recordings.

Those involved in the production of qualified film; water, natural gas, or electricity; the construction of real property; and services such as architecture and engineering (these form the DPGR receipts mentioned below).

This part of the tax code allows the deduction for those filing regular and AMT tax for individuals; farming co-operatives; estates, trusts and their beneficiaries; farming cooperatives; and is also applicable to partners and owners of S corporations (and not to partnerships or S corporations themselves).

A few definitions would be helpful in explaining this section of the TCJA (they might sound complex, but they really aren't with some reading and tax advice from a professional):

- **QPAI:** qualified production activities income. This is the net income that is generated from taxpayer's activities that qualify.

- **DPGR:** domestic production gross receipts. These are taxpayer gross receipts that qualify some of which include those activities mentioned above.

- **QPP:** qualifying production property. Is the item or good that generates revenue for the taxpayer and may potentially be considered the DPGR above.

- **MPGE:** manufactured, produced, grown or extracted. The MPGE is relevant when discussing the QPP.

The section 199 deduction (DPAD) is calculated by using the following formula:

DPGR - CGS (other expenses allocable to DPGR) = QPAI

QPAI x 9 % = DPAD

What was the problem?

As with some of the other sections in this book, there may not necessarily have been an issue with the old law. The simple explanation for this is that changes in laws, as highlighted by this change in the tax code, are dynamic. This means that some laws may be in favor of the general populace, whilst other may not. However, beyond the cold hard facts, perception of the law is that this may inhibit those companies that may have benefited from this law when it was in effect.

What does the new law do / require?

The new law is repealed for tax years after 2017, meaning that it can no longer be used in the calculation of deductions, and cannot be used to lower tax bills for those that previously qualified. In essence, the law has been repealed and thus cannot, in any way, be used in the manner that it was to begin with.

What does this mean for Jack and Jill Enterprises? (and Andreas Coffee Shop as well)

J&J may not be affected directly, and neither would Andreas, especially since neither of the two qualify for the sectors that this law encompasses. However, if any of the two were in this sector, they may not have been hard done by the law. For one, the negative impacts of the law could easily be contested as having been made up for by the lowering of the corporate tax rate. However, we do note that this law may not have been exclusively encompassing of those within the corporate world.

Misconceptions/ Criticisms/ Clarification

Companies that are involved in the technology sector benefited directly from this part of the tax code before its repeal, especially those related to manufacturing and/ or research and development (R&D) conducted within the U.S. Some of the companies include those dealing in the manufacture of semiconductors, software/ cloud companies that provide software, computer hardware/ peripherals, as well as companies that provide on-line software.

The elimination of these incentives to such companies is not necessarily all negative, especially considering that the significant drop in the corporate tax rate from 35% to 21% is likely to have a significant impact on lowering costs at these companies anyway. Therefore, taking such incentives away from them is not entirely negative, and unless computations that suggest the contrary are compiled, we suspect that the corporate rate drop is likely to make up for the incentives, and then some. In addition, the TCJA also has tax credits that are available for continued research, meaning that companies that benefited from DPAD are likely to continue benefiting from these continued research credits (EY Global Tax Alert Library, 2017).

Expert tips

Companies affected by this law should note that these laws mainly impact on cash flows and the timing of these cash flows, rather than necessarily eliminating the research credit. This means that companies affected by this law, such as those in the technology sector, will eventually find themselves in the same position they would have been before the implementation of the new law. However, this would take a longer time to realization, estimated by Ernst & Young to stand at around 5 – 15 years.

Calendar and fiscal year taxpayers may still qualify and take advantage of DPAD when filing 2017 returns. Fiscal year taxpayers are eligible to claim it for QPAI that is linked to the 2017 & 2018.

PART XI

Chapter 12 : Changes to Executive Compensation for Publicly Held Entities / Companies / Organizations — Section 162(M)

CHANGES TO EXECUTIVE COMPENSATION FOR PUBLICLY HELD ENTITIES/ COMPANIES/ ORGANIZATIONS – SECTION 162(M)

What is the law? A brief

Employers in the U.S., as with many other countries across the globe, may generally reasonably deduct compensation (to employees) for work done. Whether compensation is reasonable is usually difficult to be objective about, and thus the law steps in to regulate the amount of remuneration that an organization can deduct under compensation, limited to $1million for covered employees working for the corporation (Kaplan, 2017).

Prior to the passing of the TCJA, the law has several clauses governing it that have since been reworked in the new law. One such law is that the law allowed for deduction limitations that excluded amounts paid to employees that were characterized as 'qualified performance-based compensation'. Further, in this context, covered employees include the company's chief executive officer, as well as each of the next three most highly compensated executive officers (specific to the year in question). In addition, these rules were generally applied only to those companies whose equity securities were publicly traded (Polk, 2018).

What was the problem

The outgoing law, though noble in its formation, had several loopholes that allowed publicly held companies circumvent the limits that the law had. Some of these include retirement income from a qualified plan or annuity, commission-based compensation, qualified performance-based compensation, and also those benefits that are excluded from the executive's gross income.

If a covered individual met the targets set for them by the company's board of directors, such individuals would be due compensation that formed part of the commission for the revenue the individual may have either made or saved the company. As part of the old tax law, these would not be considered as part of executive compensation. However, as part of the new law, unless these payments are part of grandfathered contracts instituted before 2 November 2017, they would not qualify as deductibles as part of the company's overall tax liability.

What does the new law do / require?

There are several changes made by the TCJA with regard to section 162(m).

Removal of the exemption for "qualified performance-based compensation" exception

For tax years beginning after 31 December 2017, the TCJA eliminates the performance-based exception, other than those arrangements that are considered grandfathered (will be discussed as part of its own subtitle). The elimination of this exception means that payments to employees that exceed the $1million limit are not deductible and thus will be taxed separately (the excess; amounts that exceed the limit). However, there are two limits under to this, allowing for payments to be deductible even in general breach of the law. The two limits are the following:-

- A company may qualify for a deduction under a test referred to as the "all events" test, compensation that must be paid by 15 March 2018. These payments are only for those that qualify in 2017

- Grandfathered compensation contracts that are binding

Expansion of covered employees

The changes to this section of the law applies to those employees that are considered "covered". Under the outgoing law, covered employees included the principal executive officer (most likely the CEO, but may include titles such as the MD), or the three highest compensated executive officers (other than the CEO and CFO), and these deductions were required to be included as part of the company's Summary Compensation Table (SCT), according to the SEC's disclosure rules. The CFO was excluded from this list. Further, an executive officer would only be considered covered, if he or she was employed an executive officer of the company on the last day of the tax year.

Under TCJA, the CFO is expressly included as part of covered employees. Further, if an individual was employed as a covered employee at any point beginning or after 1 January 2017, the employee will be considered covered for that year and all other years that follow it, whether or not that employee is terminated. Therefore, all payments made to an employee during or after the first tax year that the employee becomes covered will be subject to the $1million deduction limit, payments of which include incentive awards, deferred compensation and severance benefits. These payments expressly qualify as covered unless they fall under the grandfathered contract exception.

Expansion of covered companies

As mentioned, the outgoing law applied only to covered employees with equity securities traded on the SEC, required to be registered under Section 12 of the Securities Exchange Act of 1934. Our guidance on the companies that may be considered as covered companies under the TCJA is to consult tax and legal counsel as they would be best placed to advise.

However, some of the corporations included in the new law are those with publicly traded debt and foreign companies publicly traded through American depositary receipts. As part of the old law, foreign private issuers were not subject to the deduction limitation, but these are now included.

Grandfathered contracts

Grandfather contracts are those that are written and legally binding between an employer and the employee. In the case of this law, grandfathered contracts (employment contracts) would suffice for exemption, but only if the employer accepts that they do not have the right to amend the plan materially, or terminate the plan once they have received exemption on it.

The binding contract would need to be determined as existing, and specifically enforced before 2 November 2017. Further, the company needs to assess whether the employed individual would prevail if they sought to enforce the payment of compensation as prescribed by the contract itself, and employment law. Any right to terminate or materially amend the contract would indicate that it does not qualify to be grandfathered.

It should be noted that severance payments are now included, if those payments were not included in employee contracts before the new law was instituted. Under the new "once a covered employee, always a covered employee" clause, severance payments agreed to as part of a written binding contract and put in place prior to the 2 November 2017 deadline are not subject to the $1million deduction limit. This also applies to any other compensation benefits that may exceed the limit that were entered into before the deadline date (EY, 2017).

IPO transition period

The IPO transition period section of the law consists of regulations that provide a transition period for those privately held companies that become public. Similar to grandfathered contracts, the $1million deduction limit does not apply to any remuneration paid as part of a compensation plan or agreement that was already in place prior to the company going public. For companies that go public through an initial public offering (IPO), there exists a transition period in which the deduction limitations do not apply, and in this case, the period would last until the first shareholder meeting that takes place in the third calendar year after the IPO. Essentially, the period lasts for 3 years post IPO. However, for those companies that become public as a result of being separated from a public company (spin off), the period in question is shortened to 12 months (Polk, 2018).

What does this mean for Jack and Jill Enterprises? (and Andreas Coffee Shop as well)

This law is specific to publicly traded companies, and as such, may not necessarily apply to J&J or Andreas as currently described. However, should any of these individuals go on to either constitute a part of the board of directors of a publicly traded company, or become an executive officer, they would be best advised to familiarize themselves with these laws as they would directly affect them.

Misconceptions/ Criticisms/ Clarification

The "all events" test is one that specifies those conditions that must be fulfilled before the end of the tax year in question. If a company meets the criteria specified, it is eligible to deduct compensation for that tax year, even if the payment for these deductions is expected to be done in the following year. This exception, limited to the first quarter of 2018 only (as discussed earlier – under section (c) above), means that a company will be able to deduct the compensation that qualifies from 2017, in 2018. As mentioned earlier, these payments must be made by 15 March 2018.

The new law also closes the "employed till the last day" loophole, meaning that those executive officers are covered by the company.

Expert tips

The elimination of the performance-based exception allows leaders within such companies increased flexibility in how creatively they can structure their performance-based compensation arrangements. The outgoing law provided strict requirements for exceptions under performance-based compensation, specifically around how performance goals were set and approved in order to increase compensation to employees.

Such structuring may include replacing awards such as stock options and stock appreciation rights with other forms of incentive compensation. Further, companies will have to consider the impact of the reduction of the corporate tax rate from 35% to 21%, especially considering the effect that the reduced tax rate may have on performance metrics, and whether those performance metrics will be permitted or would require adjustment.

Employers that fall under this category of the law may be required to conduct an inventory of the executive compensation they may have in place, including compensation committee charters, and consider updating them in the wake of this law, with the assistance of tax and legal counsel. Finally, employers will also be best served if they ensure that those grandfathered arrangements that were installed before 2 November 2017 are in compliance with the performance-based exception, and that they are not materially modified in a way that will likely cause them to lose their grandfathered status. A loss of this status is likely to cause a failure to comply with the exemption, forcing the company to comply with the new law, thus losing the advantages that the grandfathered status would have afforded them (Nealon & Ostrower, 2018).

PART XII

Chapter 13 : New Measures of Inflation

NEW MEASURE OF INFLATION

What is the law? A brief

No, this does not mean that we are about to start a statistics class. However, understanding how the government recognizes inflation is crucial. The reason this is so is because inflation, and how the government calculates it, affects how your tax brackets are calculated.

The CPI – Consumer Price Index – is a common measure of how the cost of living goes up (inflation) or down (deflation). As is the case with many of these units of measure, the CPI comes in many variants, and one of the variants that the federal government introduced into the TCJA intends to fill some of the gaps to the federal budget caused by some of the tax cuts introduced by the law. One of the ways that the government intends to do this is by introducing a variant to the CPI known as the chained CPI (Chandra, 2017).

The chained CPI, like the traditional CPI, is reported annually by the U.S. Labor Department's Bureau of Labor Statistics, reports that include and track the prices of around 80,000 different goods and services purchased by consumers within urban settings/ areas. However, the chain CPI uses what is known a substitution bias, essentially recognizing that consumers tend to shift their decisions on the items to purchase by comparing the prices of related items. This can be explained by consumers switching brands of soft drinks if the price of one of the products rises in relation to another. By only measuring the increases in the prices of goods and services by using the chained CPI, the inflation of goods and services rises slower than traditional CPI would.

What was the problem

Traditional CPI rises faster, because the CPI assumes that the market basket specific to a household does not change relative to the rise in prices, which is not necessarily true. As explained above, households are more likely to substitute the products they use in order to keep their relative spending at the same level. Therefore, chained CPI measures inflation by assuming that these households are more likely to substitute those products with significant rises in price (Motley, 1997).

Because inflation is a measure of the cost of living relative to the general population, faster rises in inflation are likely to cancel any gains that workers might make through increased salaries or higher revenues in business. This is because inflation is likely to make the rises in their earnings smaller, because inflation raises the prices of goods and services, thus making these items more expensive relative to any gains made in earnings. Basically, a slower measure of inflation suggests that workers can buy more items in these baskets relative to the rise in the cost.

What does the new law do / require?

Here's the interpretation. Traditionally, the government has used the traditional CPI to adjust the income tax brackets with which they use to tax citizens. The new law shifts from the use of traditional CPI in order to make adjustments to tax brackets, to using chained CPI. The best way to think about this is by using average earnings for a single worker, say Joe, over a period of time. If for example, a worker, say Jane, earned $ 35,000 in 2003, and that this worker receives pay increases of 0.4% due to steady inflation throughout the years. In 2018, Jane would now receive $ 39,440 (assuming that the pay rises are only due to inflation). Consider also the tax brackets as per the below table:

Tax brackets	
Singles	
Taxable Income	**Tax Rate**
$0 - $9,325	10% of taxable income
$9,326 - $37,950	$932.50 + 15% of the amount over $9,325
$37,951 - $91,900	$5,226.25 + 25% of the amount over $37,950
$91,901 - $191,650	$18,713.75 + 28% of the amount over $91,900
$191,651 - $416,700	$46,643.75 + 33% of the amount over $191,650
$416,701 - $418,400	$120,910.25 + 35% of the amount over $416,700
$418,401 or more	$121,505.25 + 39.6% of the amount over $418,400

Source: TCJA

If the government does not change the taxable income brackets above over time, then Jane will move from the income bracket of $ 9,326 - $ 37,950 to $ 37,951 - $ 91,900, essentially having to pay more taxes.

Companies make adjustments to salaries and worker pay based on traditional CPI, thus making adjustments to try and ensure that the workers are able to retain the same amount of value for their money as relates to inflation.

What does this mean for Jack and Jill Enterprises? (and Andreas Coffee Shop as well)

The effect of this on J&J and Andreas is difficult to establish because there are several factors that contribute towards rises in earnings. However, as established above, the use of the chained CPI is likely to raise taxpayers into higher tax brackets, especially since the tax cuts instituted by the TCJA will end in 2025. Thereafter, the chained CPI will continue to be used as the standard with which tax brackets are revised. This will likely mean that taxpayers will experience higher taxes, especially after the tax cuts currently in place are ended (Chandra, 2017).

Misconceptions/ Criticisms/ Clarification

The use of chained CPI to calculate tax brackets means that taxpayers, over time, are likely to pay more taxes without necessarily increasing their real income (the actual amount of money that they have). The TCJA was heralded as a tax break for everybody. However, assuming that things stay the same, in a decade or so, taxpayers will pay more taxes, with corporations likely paying the same taxes that they are paying now. The common taxpayer is therefore going to see their taxes increased whilst corporations enjoy breaks (Chandra, 2017).

However, the argument for reducing corporation taxes has not been one that argues for equity, but instead one that acts as an overall economic stimulus. This means that these changes in chained CPI, even if they do not necessarily increase the overall income for taxpayers, will be offset by improvement in the country's economic performance. Think of it as the GOP hoping to achieve several levels of collections for the IRS, all the while maintaining a balance based on what each stakeholder considers beneficial enough to keep them happy. Remember that politics is not always about doing what is right, but what is possible. Congress is party affiliated, and Congressmen and Congresswomen have to be accountable not only to their party and donors, but also to the electorate. Finding this balance can be difficult to achieve, especially when considering contentious issues such a tax plan. This is perhaps not the strongest argument in favor of the tax plan, but it is the argument presented at the present time.

Expert tips

The typical difference between traditional CPI and chained CPI, though small at a glance, can be significant over time. Over time, it adds up, as highlighted by the graph below that shows the increase in traditional CPI when compared to chained CPI. Over a period, the difference in growth between the two is around 6 percentage points. This is most likely to have an effect on the tax levied on individuals.

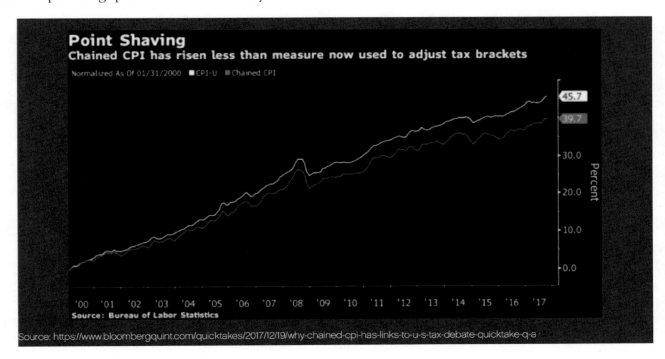

Source: https://www.bloombergquint.com/quicktakes/2017/12/19/why-chained-cpi-has-links-to-u-s-tax-debate-quicktake-q-a

PART XIII

Chapter 14 : Doubling of the Expensing Limit Under Section 179

DOUBLING OF THE EXPENSING LIMIT UNDER SECTION 179

What is the law? A brief

Depreciating an asset is standard practice in the business world because capital assets either gain or lose value. Those assets that lose value are depreciated in order to match their true value. As such, in order for the government to incentivise businesses to replace their current depreciating asset bases, the government acts to increase the amount of depreciation that a business can charge on its net income. Businesses can therefore use their overall lower tax charge to replace the assets that are depreciating in value and use.

Section 179 of the tax law addresses those properties used in a business or other income-generating activity. Changes to the way these properties are recognized and depreciated has a direct influence on the amount of capital assets that a business can acquire. If the tax law allows for significant levels of depreciation, the effect on a company's financials is likely to be positive. This is because allowing depreciation means that this cost can deducted from the net taxable income, meaning that it is likely to lower the overall liability that a business may face (SC&H Group, 2018).

A reduction in the amount of depreciation that a business can charge on its assets means that said business is likely to increase the overall amount of taxes paid, leaving the business with lower levels of cash. This will likely dis-incentivise the business towards capital assets, choosing instead to invest in other assets with higher incentives. Further, this is not likely to spur economic growth due to lower investment in capital assets. An increase in the depreciable percentage a business can charge is likely to lead to lower tax charges on businesses due to lowered net taxable income. This is therefore likely to incentivise business to improve their capital asset base due to the incentive to invest in them due to the lower tax charge, thus improving the capital base of the economy. A larger capital asset base is likely to improve the revenue generating capabilities of an economy.

What was the problem

The previous law had two broader issues with it. For one, there was used assets were not allowable for deductions, meaning that the law lacked incentive for those assets that held potential/ opportunity for additional value add to the economy. In addition to this, these assets were subject only to a 50% deduction on their value at cost. Though not necessarily a problem, an increase to the value of the deduction would likely spur growth by incentivising people and businesses to invest in assets that fall under this class.

What does the new law do / require?

This law allows for the immediate deduction of 100% of the cost of certain qualified property that is acquired and placed in service before 1 January 2023. Under the old law, depreciation deduction had been scheduled to end in 2019, which has been adjusted upwards to 2026 (2027 for certain aircraft and production period property). The old law only allowed for a 50% allowance for depreciation on property that has now increased to 100% for property that has been placed in service after 27 September 2017 and before 1

January 2023. Longer production period property and certain aircraft qualify for this depreciation to extend to 1 January 2024, as well as specified plants planted or grafted after 27 September 2017 and before 1 January 2023 (Johnson, 2017).

What does this mean for Jack and Jill Enterprises? (and Andreas Coffee Shop as well)

The short life of the depreciation and expensing rule may lead to the creation of an incentive that may drive taxpayers to acquire assets that are eligible for immediate expensing. Such investments in assets (over consumption of products without much underlying value) is intended to spur economic growth due to increased trade in such-like assets. Therefore, if J&J invested in assets that qualified under the depreciation rule, and amounting to $20,000 in cost value, the table below shows their tax calculations under the old depreciation bonus rate and the new one.

Comparison of old versus new bonus depreciable rate

J&J - Old depreciable rate		J&J - New depreciable rate	
Net income	$ 120,000	Net income	$ 120,000
Asset value	$ 20,000	Asset value	$ 20,000
50% deduction	$ 10,000	100% deduction	$ 20,000
New net income	$ 110,000	New net income	$ 100,000
Payable	$ 10,452.5	Payable	$ 10,452.5
Excess	$ 34,099	Excess	$ 24,099
Tax	$ 8,525	Tax	$ 6,025
Total tax	$ 18,977	Total tax	$ 16,477
Net tax savings		$ 2,500	

Source: computation

If J&J invested in a qualifying asset of $20,000, they would experience net savings of around $2,500. The savings are impacted most by the doubling of the deduction rate from 50% to 100%, meaning that the entire $20,000 is deductible on the couple's net income, a situation that was not possible under the previous regime. Further, it should also be noted that if the couple bought an asset of higher depreciable value, not only will the asset reduce their overall taxable income before calculation of standard deductions. The effect of purchases of higher value items is highlighted below:

Comparison of lower cost and higher cost asset

J&J - Lower cost asset		J&J - Higher cost asset	
Net income	$ 120,000	Net income	$ 120,000
Asset value	$ 20,000	Asset value	$ 50,000
100% deduction	$ 20,000	100% deduction	$ 50,000
New net income	$ 100,000	New net income	$ 70,000
Payable	$ 10,452.5	Payable	$ 1,865.0
Excess	$ 24,099	Excess	$ 51,349
Tax	$ 6,025	Tax	$ 7,702
Total tax	$ 16,477	Total tax	$ 9,567
Net tax savings		$ 6,910	

The table above builds on the previous one, with the computation only changing with regards to the cost value of the qualifying asset. If the asset value is increased to $50,000, the result is a lower standard deduction due to taxable income reducing from the $100,000 to $70,000, dropping the couple from one income tax bracket to a lower one, meaning that their standard deduction also falls. Further, the tax on the excess amounts of income in their new tax bracket is lower, meaning that they pay a lower tax amount of $9,567. Overall, the couple would save $6,910 for the year on this section of the TCJA.

Misconceptions/ Criticisms/ Clarification

Under the previous law (concerning bonus depreciation), a taxpayer was only able to deduct up to 50% first year bonus depreciation. In addition, used assets did not qualify and thus the law was only applicable for the cost of new vehicles, equipment, machinery, office furniture, equipment etc. The TCJA also allows for 100% depreciation for film, live theatrical productions and television that qualify and were placed in service on or after 28 September 2017.

The misconception here might be with the applicability of the law (used assets are allowed in calculation of the bonus depreciation) as well as the time limits concerned. It should also be noted that this bonus depreciation, beginning in 2023, is scheduled to be reduced by 20 percentage points every year until its final elimination in 2027 (Rossitto & Associates, 2018).

It should be noted, however, that each asset class is allowable for a specific amount of depreciation. Consult your tax consultant for schedules on these depreciable amounts per asset class. Examples used herein are generic to show the overall effect of the change in the law on businesses.

Expert tips

You should consider investing, should you have access to such funds, in those assets that qualify under the bonus depreciation. Further, those of you that purchased said assets on or after 28 September 2017 should consult a tax consultant or accountant in order to take advantage of this bonus as it is likely to significantly impact overall tax obligations (through calculation).

Such is likely to happen by deductions made on taxable income for the year, made by deducting 100% of the value (cost) of said asset.

As mentioned in section XI, the state and local property tax cannot be prepaid with the express intention of avoiding limits on the $10,000 amount. To recap, individuals can only determine whether a deduction of this nature is allowed as it depends on whether the taxpayer made the payment in the year and whether those payments were assessed in the same year.

Therefore, prepayments made but not assessed are not deductible in the year intended, but only deductible when they are assessed.

PART XIV

Chapter 15 : Other Provisions

OTHER PROVISIONS

What is the law? A brief

In this section, we shall attempt to cover those provisions that may not have been discussed as parts of previous sections. As earlier intimated, there does not exist a specific section of the TCJA that specifies provisions that fall under 'other provisions'.

Conversely, these provisions shall be selected by order of significance and relayed to you, the reader, in order to potentially inform you on some of the changes (or some of those important topics that remained untouched) therein. These provisions are also likely to be broad and touch on many areas of the law.

Some of the provisions that we will discuss herein are:

- Elimination of the personal casualty and theft loss deduction

- State and local income, and property tax

- New tax credit for employer-paid family and medical leave

- Limitations on deductions for employee fringe benefits

What was the problem

The drafters of the TCJA would have wanted to achieve as much as possible with the tax change bill. For that reason, a number of isolated provisions can be found. There may not be any specific issues with the laws to be discussed. However, we will detail the changes to the laws if any, and how these are likely to affect those businesses and individuals targeted by this law.

What does the new law do / require?

Elimination of the personal casualty and theft loss deduction

Under the prior tax law, if an individual suffered an uncompensated loss that arose from a fire, ship-wreck, storm, earthquake, wildfires, weather (events such as hurricanes or tornadoes), theft, and others, the individual was allowed to deduct this loss as part of their itemized deductions. Under the new TCJA law, losses incurred before 1 January 2026 are only deductible if they arise in an area that is federally declared as a disaster area. All other losses of this nature are not allowable for deductions.

State and local income, and property tax

As discussed as part of section XI of this report, there is a limitation on the individuals making per-payments on state and local income taxes, it should be noted that firstly, individuals may deduct up to $10,000 in the form of state and local taxes. These include income, sales and property tax, and can be deducted from your taxable income annually, with limitations on their application (Rice, 2018).

New tax credit for employer-paid family and medical leave

For the years beginning 1 January 2018 and ending 31 December 2019, the TCJA has created a federal tax credit applicable to employers that paid for and provided family and medical leave to their employees. As part of this incentive, eligible employers are able to claim a general business credit that is equal to a percentage of wages paid to employees who qualify for leave under the Family and Medical Leave Act. Further, companies can only receive the credit if they are able to cater for at least 50% of an employee's regular earnings, as wells as at least two weeks of leave.

The credit ranges from 12.5 – 25% of hourly cost of paid leave. This means that the government will cover the 12.5% of the benefits the worker receives whilst on leave if the employer provides half of the employee's earnings. The cost covered by the government will then rise to 25% if the workers receive their entire earnings (Miller, 2018).

Limitations on deductions for employee fringe benefits

Fringe benefits are those benefits that are afforded to an employee in order to supplement their traditional money wages or salary. Such benefits may include a company car (personal use), group-term life insurance cover, employee stock options, employee discounts and others. The prior law provided for the exclusion of qualified transportation fringe benefits from gross income, with the benefit including "transportation in a commuter highway vehicle if such transportation is in connection with travel between the employee's residence and place of employment", qualified parking expenses, transit passes and "qualified bicycle commuting reimbursement" costs.

The TCJA repeals the prior law's employer deduction for qualified mass transit and parking benefits, except for those that are deemed necessary for ensuring the safety of an employee. The repeal also includes the exclusion of qualified bicycle commuting reimbursements from gross income and wages for the period beginning after 31 December 2017 and before 1 January 2026.

The TCJA also repeals most of the rules around deductions for amusement, entertainment or recreation that is associated directly with the company (Bianchi, 2018).

What does this mean for Jack and Jill Enterprises? (and Andreas Coffee Shop as well)

Jack and Jill, as well as Andreas, will not be eligible for itemized deductions that would have been allowed under the prior law for loss of property through causes discussed herein. Therefore, they are best served by analyzing the risk associated with the area in which they live, as well as discussing options that would secure their assets in the event of such property loss.

J&J and Andreas can now feel a little better about paying for leave (annual or medical) given the introduction of deductions for the same. Further, this is likely to impact positively with employees, raising their morale in the process.

J&J and Andreas will no longer be able to deduct any fringe benefits from their gross income. The extent of this will be difficult to ascertain due to the size of the tax cut to the overall corporate tax rate. Given that fringe benefits are likely insignificant when computing the overall effect of the law on a company's tax costs, the significant reduction to the corporate tax rate is likely to cover for the loss of fringe benefits deductions.

Misconceptions/ Criticisms/ Clarification

Areas that are not declared as disaster areas, but experience federally designated disasters qualify for tax breaks under the personal casualty and theft loss deduction. Therefore, for example, those affected by the hurricane Harvey and Irma, as well as those that were affected by wildfires that razed significant portions of Northern Californian wine country, would qualify for the deductions. However, as stated, these deductions only apply for those that are affected by federally recognized disasters.

One criticism of the repeal of the law is that it excludes those that experience similar tragedies, such as the Southern Californian wildfires, fires that affected individuals in one large geographical area, but divided by further boundaries. These individuals may feel hard done by the classification by the federal classification of the disaster (Bell, 2017).

Expert tips

Individuals that live or work outside of federally declared disaster areas should look at acquiring property insurance coverage on owned property considered valuable. In doing so, one should also consider the making records of all the items covered under the proposed insurance coverage, with advisement to take video recordings of the assets in question, as well as noting down serial numbers of electronic equipment and furniture.

Employers should also note that the tax credit for paid leave can only be applied for those workers that have been employed at the company for at least a year, and in addition, is only applicable for those workers that earned no more than $72,000 in 2017. This wage ceiling will be adjusted upwards or downwards in relation to inflation at the time. Companies can also claim the tax credit for full and part time workers if they have been employed for at least a year.

Bibliography

Bibliography

A

Anderson Kill. (2018, January 16)

Tax Bill Signed into Law

Retrieved from ://www.andersonkill.com/Publication-Details/PublicationId/1612

B

Bell, K. (2017, December 8)

Casualty loss tax deduction elimination fires up some California lawmakers

Retrieved from ://www.dontmesswithtaxes.com/2017/12/casualty-loss-tax-deduction-fires-up-some-california-lawmakers.html

Bianchi, A. J. (2018, January 3)

The Impact of the Tax Cuts and Jobs Act on Employee and Fringe Benefits

Retrieved from ://www.natlawreview.com/article/impact-tax-cuts-and-jobs-act-employee-and-fringe-benefits

Boaz, D. (2001, February 28)

One Bad and Eight Good Reasons to Cut Taxes

Retrieved from ://www.cato.org/publications/commentary/one-bad-eight-good-reasons-cut-taxes

Bowman, S. (2017, November 9)

Full Expensing: The Best Idea in Politics You've Never Heard Of

Retrieved from ://www.adamsmith.org/blog/full-expensing-the-best-idea-in-politics-youve-never-heard-of

Burkett & Burkett. (2018, September 1)

TCJA Makes Changes to '529 Plans'

Retrieved from ://burkettcpas.com/tcja-makes-changes/

Burman, L. E., Nunns, J. R., Page, B. R., Rohaly, J., & Rosenburg, J. (2017)

An Analysis of the House GOP Tax Plan

Columbia Journal of Tax Law, 8(2), pp. 258-294

C

Carmichael, S. G. (2012, March 15)

America's Education Problem

Retrieved from ://hbr.org/2012/03/americas-education-problem

Center on Budget and Policy Priorities - CBPP. (2017, October 10)

Corporate Rate Cuts Are a Poor Way to Help the Economy and Most Workers - and Could Hurt Them

Retrieved from ://www.cbpp.org/research/federal-tax/corporate-rate-cuts-are-a-poor-way-to-help-the-economy-and-most-workers-and

Chandra, S. (2017, November 20)

What You Need to Know About 'Chained CPI'

Retrieved from ://www.bloomberg.com/news/articles/2017-11-20/why-chained-cpi-has-links-to-u-s-tax-debate-quicktake-q-a

Clemens, J. (2018, January 15)

How the Tax Cuts & Jobs Act (TCJA) Will Affect Individuals and Businesses

Retrieved from ://www.wisdomws.com/tcja-wisdom-wealth-strategies-denver-financial-planner/

Committee for a Responsible Federal Budget - CFRB. (2017, November 2)

Tax Cuts and Jobs Act Will Cost $ 1.5 Trillion

Retrieved from ://www.crfb.org/blogs/tax-cut-and-jobs-act-will-cost-15-trillion

Corporate Direct. (2017, December 14)

Estate and Gift Tax Exemptions Increased for 2018

Retrieved from ://www.corporatedirect.com/blog/estate-and-gift-tax-exemptions-increased/

D

Dillon, P., & Hobbs, M. (2018, January 18)

Untangling tax reform: business losses and NOLs for corporate and noncorporate tax-payers

Retrieved from ://bakertilly.com/insights/untangling-tax-reform-business-losses-and-nols-for-corporate-and-noncorpora

E

EY. (2017, December 20)

Conference Agreement on the "Tax Cuts and Jobs Act" includes significant executive compensation and employee benefits provisions

Retrieved from ://taxnews.ey.com/news/2017-2160-conference-agreement-on-the-tax-cuts-and-job s-act-includes-significant-executive-compensation-and-employee-benefits-provisions

EY Global Tax Alert Library. (2017)

US Tax Cuts and Jobs Act and its impact on technology sector

Retrieved from ://www.ey.com/Publication/vwLUAssets/US_Tax_Cuts_and_Jobs_Act_and_its_im-pact_on_technology_sector/$FILE/2017G_07175-171Gbl_US%20TCJA%20and%20its%20im-pact%20on%20technology%20sector.pdf

F

Floyd, D. (2018, January 12)

Trump's Tax Reform Plan

Retrieved from ://www.investopedia.com/news/trumps-tax-reform-what-can-be-done/

Fontinelle, A. (2018, January 3)

How the GOP Tax Bill Affects You

Retrieved from ://www.investopedia.com/taxes/how-gop-tax-bill-affects-you/

G

Graham & Dunn - Estate Planning Advisor. (2011, May, 17)

Wealth Transfer Tax System

Retrieved from ://www.millernash.com/wealth-transfer-tax-system-05-17-2011/

Greenburg, S. (2017, January 17)

Pass-Through Businesses: Data and Policy

Retrieved from ://taxfoundation.org/pass-through-businesses-data-and-policy/

H

Hamilton Tharp LLP. (2017, December 22)

Tax Reforms - Key Changes Summary

Retrieved from ://ht2cpa.com/wp-content/uploads/2017/12/Tax-Reform-Key-Changes-Summary-22DEC17.pdf

Hartsock, W.D. (2013)

Contesting an IRS Levy

Retrieved from ://thetaxlawyer.com/tax-collections/information/contesting-irs-levy

I

IRS. (n.d.)

Collection Appeal Rights

Retrieved from ://www.irs.gov/pub/irs-pdf/p1660.pdf

J

Johnson, C. (2017)

Tax Cuts and Jobs Act of 2017: Summary of Provisions Impacting Businesses

Retrieved from ://www.silvercreekteam.com/wp-content/uploads/2017/12/Tax-Cuts-and-Jobs-Act-of-2017-Business-Provisions.pdf

K

Kliff, S. (2015, July 2)

Obamacare's Individual Mandate, explained

Retrieved from ://www.vox.com/cards/individual-mandate/what-is-individual-mandate

Krieg, G. (2017, December 4)

Two quotes form GOP senators explain the GOP tax bill

Retrieved from ://edition.cnn.com/2017/12/04/politics/chuck-grassley-orrin-hatch-explain-republican-tax-cuts/index.html

Krupkin, A., & Looney, A. (2017, May 15)

9 facts about pass-through businesses

Retrieved from ://www.brookings.edu/research/9-facts-about-pass-through-businesses/

Kaplan, D. M. (2017, December 19)

Tax Reform Bill Tightens $ 1M Limit on Deductibility of Pubic Company Executive Compensation

Retrieved from ://www.pepperlaw.com/publications/tax-reform-bill-tightens-1m-limit-on-deductibility-of-public-company-executive-compensation-2017-12-19/

KPMG. (2015)

Section 199: Domestic Production Activities Deduction

Retrieved from ://assets.kpmg.com/content/dam/kpmg/pdf/2015/07/388512_Section199_DomesticProduction_WEB.pdf

L

Lobosco, K. (2017, December 20)

Why the GOP tax bill is a win for DeVos' agenda

Retrieved from ://money.cnn.com/2017/12/20/pf/private-school-529-tax-bill/index.html

Miller, S. (2018, January 11)

Taking Advantage of the New Paid-Leave Tax Credit

Retrieved from ://www.shrm.org/resourcesandtools/hr-topics/benefits/pages/taking-advantage-of-paid-leave-tax-credit.aspx

Mitchell, N., & Greenburg, J. (2018, January 10)

What the new tax law means for your 2018 finances

Retrieved from ://wtop.com/business-finance/2018/01/what-the-new-tax-law-means-for-your-2018-taxes/

Motley, B. (1997, May 23)

FRBSF Economic Letter

Retrieved from ://www.frbsf.org/economic-research/publications/economic-letter/1997/may/bias-in-the-cpi-roughly-right-or-precisely-wrong/#subs

N

Nealon, A., & Ostrower, M. (2018, January 5)

2018 Tax Reform Series: Executive Compensation Changes for Publicly Held Entities

Retrieved from ://www.natlawreview.com/article/2018-tax-reform-series-executive-compensation-changes-publicly-held-entities

O

Ozimek, A. (2017, January 12)

The Case Against Cutting Top Marginal Tax Rates

Retrieved from ://www.economy.com/dismal/analysis/datapoints/292435/The-Case-Against-Cutting-Top-Marginal-Tax-Rates/

P

Pickering, K. (2017, December 20)

How the Tax Cuts and Jobs Act impacts U.S. tax returns

Retrieved from ://www.hrblock.com/tax-center/irs/tax-reform/tax-cuts-and-jobs-act/

Polk, D. (2018, January 31)

Administering Compensation Programs in the Wake of the Tax Cuts and Jobs Act - New Section 162(m)

Retrieved from ://www.davispolk.com/files/2018-01-31_administering_compensation_programs_in_wake_of_tcja_new_section_162m.pdf

Pomerleau, K. (2015, January 21)

An Overview of Pass-Through Businesses in the United States

Retrieved from ://taxfoundation.org/overview-pass-through-businesses-united-states/

pWc. (2017)

Corporate - Taxes on corporate income

Retrieved from ://taxsummaries.pwc.com/ID/United-States-Corporate-Taxes-on-corporate-income

R

Rice, L. (2018, January 2)

Key Provisions in the Final Tax Reform Bill Affecting Individuals

Retrieved from ://www.lexology.com/library/detail.aspx?g=4c35c08c-e489-480e-a419-8be-5ab562d6b

Rossitto & Associates. (2018, January 30)

Changes to Meal, Entertainment and Transportation Deductions

Retrieved from ://www.rossittoassoc.com/blog/

Rugy, V. (2011, July 11)

How Much of Federal Spending is Borrowed for Every Dollar

Retrieved from ://www.mercatus.org/publication/how-much-federal-spending-borrowed-every-dollar

S

SCH&H Group. (2018, January 11)

2018 Tax Roadmap: Depreciation Changes Under Tax Reform

Retrieved from ://www.schgroup.com/resource/blog-post/depreciation-changes-tax-reform/

Shamoun, R. (2013, December 21)

Contesting an IRS Levy

Retrieved from ://www.irssolution.com/contesting-an-irs-levy/

T

Tax and Job Cuts Act of 2017, H.R.1 - 115th.

Tax and Policy Centre Briefing Book (2016)

Key Elements of the U.S. Tax System

Retrieved from ://www.taxpolicycenter.org/briefing-book/what-amt

Tax Debt Help. (2017)

Appealing an IRS Tax Levy: When and How to Request

Retrieved from ://www.taxdebthelp.com/tax-problems/tax-levy/appeal

Tax Debt Help. (2017)

IRS Offer in Compromise: Settling Taxes For Less

Retrieved from ://www.taxdebthelp.com/tax-settlement/offer-in-compromise

Thoma, M. (2009, February 11)

Tax Cuts vs. Government Spending

Retrieved from ://economistsview.typepad.com/economistsview/2009/02/tax-cuts-vs-government-spending.html

U

U.S. Securities and Exchange Commission - Investor Publications. (2017, December 4)

An Introduction to 529 Plans

Retrieved from ://www.sec.gov/reportspubs/investor-publications/investorpubsintro529htm.html

US Tax Centre - IRS (n.d.)

Understanding how income taxes work

Retrieved from ://www.irs.com/articles/income-tax

US Tax Centre - IRS (n.d.)

2016 Federal Tax Rates, Personal Exemptions, and Standard Deductions: IRS Tax Brackets and Deduction Amounts for Tax Year 2016

Retrieved from ://www.irs.com/articles/2016-federal-tax-rates-personal-exemptions-and-standard-deductions

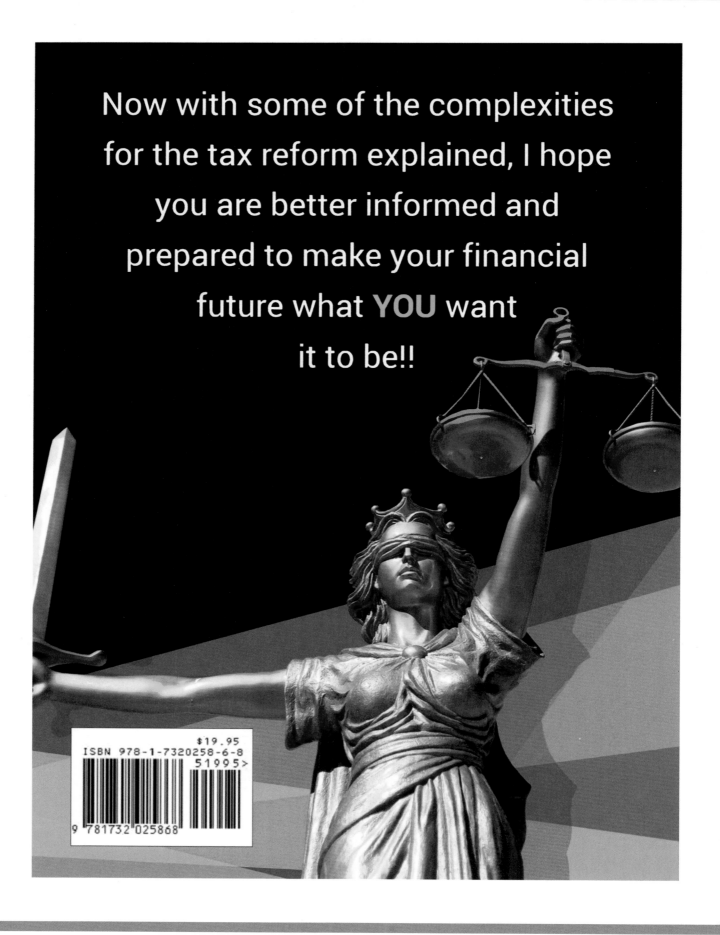

Now with some of the complexities for the tax reform explained, I hope you are better informed and prepared to make your financial future what **YOU** want it to be!!

$19.95
ISBN 978-1-7320258-6-8
51995>
9 781732 025868